RUDHIRA

THE SACRED BURNT BLOOD

DR SANJHNA NAYARR, PHD (TND)

Made with ♥ on the Notion Press Platform
www.notionpress.com

I dedicaticate this book

To the Almighty for guiding my steps, lighting my path,
and granting me the grace to complete this journey.

To my mother,
who first taught me the sacred bond between a woman and her body,
guiding me through life's cycles with tenderness and wisdom.
Your strength, love, and understanding have shaped me in ways words can't capture.

To my father,
my friend, mentor, and biggest support during every stage of life—
thank you for standing by me through every challenge, even during the times I thought I'd face them alone. Your unwavering love has meant the world.

To my daughter,
may you embrace every part of yourself with pride and grace,
knowing that these changes connect us through generations.
Your journey is just beginning, but you are never alone—
you carry within you the strength of the women who came before.

To my son,
for teaching me the purest essence of love.
You've inspired me to nurture an understanding and sensitive man,
and for that, I am forever grateful. Your compassion and heart give me hope for a brighter future.

To my fur daughters,
whose unconditional love and gentle presence have filled my life with joy and comfort.
You remind me every day of the beauty in loyalty, companionship, and the simple joys in life. Ginger, Fibi; mumma misses you dearly and know for sure that y'all have always encouraged me throughout my journey.

To all the women who have crossed my path,
thank you for your wisdom, strength, and resilience. Each of you has left an imprint on my heart, teaching me more about courage, compassion, and what it means to be a woman in this world.

Last but not the least, To the love of my life,
for your unwavering support, your endless belief in me, and the love that fills every corner of my heart. You are my strength, my partner, and my greatest joy.

Contents

Foreword

"Down"? Only Way To Go Is Up!

Growing up in India while being of a female persuasion can be the best of times and the worst of times. And sometime both at the same time.

My mom designed and sewed all our dresses while I was growing up with my three sisters. Being naturally artistically inclined, she certainly had a joyful time exploring and expanding her creativity on the four of us. Needless to say, thanks to her, we always looked pretty and well-dressed and sometimes even well-behaved to the outsiders. However, as anyone who has a family would tell you, looks are always not what they seem. The other side of that beautiful coin is usually something that none of us want to address or sometimes even acknowledge.

We were five women and girls of various ages, all growing up in one household with my dad. At any time of the month at least one of us would become "Down". That's what we called it back then.

Just as in a lot of families around the world, actually communicating and talking about it would sometimes lead to a conglomeration of emotions mixed with confusion mostly due to misinformation.

"Why is She not feeling anything when she's having her periods and I am feeling so much pain? It's not fair! Maybe something is wrong with Me!!!

Unfortunately, in some cases, adulthood may not necessarily be a time when things get better either. Some of us experience a severe case of endometriosis that can culminate in hysterectomy. My journey was somewhat similar. One saving grace was that I slowly but surely started recognizing my true soul friends and family. Eventually, I began giving myself the courage to put aside those who truly didn't care to understand me and what I was going through.

Looking back today, in my fifties, in the middle of menopause, I have only deep admiration and respect for my younger self along with a deep sense of gratitude for those who have stood by me through my sojourn.

¨Hot Flashes!!! Ha!! You don´t scare me! I have conquered months of having Fibroids and years of passing clots with excruciating and debilitating pain.

¨ To the few friends back then who would genuinely empathize with me even when they were not experiencing it themselves, I would explain to them that I had only 3 weeks every month. The 4th week, I had to sacrifice to the pain Gods! Today, I feel like I am dancing and flying because I have 4 and sometimes 5 weeks to celebrate my life every month.

In conclusion, to anyone who feels that they are in a deep hole, in horrible pain, or in depression, I want to leave you with this Mantra to uplift you from Your worst of times:

I love myself more than anyone alive.
I love my beautiful body even when I strive. I
love my hurt and know I´ll surely revive.
I love my life as I watch myself thrive.

- Anu Nadimpalli
Artist. Poet. Entrepreneur.
Founder / CEO 3AM Inspirations

ANU NADIMPALLI

Preface

Have you ever wondered if our revered Goddesses, the divine manifestations of Shakti, also experienced menstruation? I know this might raise a few eyebrows—after all, menstruation is often considered an impure subject, so how could we possibly associate it with PARASHAKTI? Sounds unthinkable, right?"

"Menstruation is a natural process experienced by girls, yet it remains shrouded in taboos and myths that often marginalize women from various social and cultural activities. In India, this subject is still largely taboo, and these deeply ingrained beliefs have a detrimental effect on the emotional well-being, mindset, lifestyle, and, most importantly, the health of girls and women. The challenge of addressing these socio-cultural taboos is compounded by the limited knowledge many girls have about puberty, menstruation, and reproductive health. Thus, a thoughtful and strategic approach is necessary to effectively address these issues. It is crucial to examine the menstruation-related myths in India and worldwide, their impact on women's lives, the importance of tackling these concerns in primary care, and strategies to overcome them."

Sadly, patriarchal societies have long influenced perceptions of menstruation, often resulting in the oppression of women and girls by stigmatizing and controlling their bodies. Globally, menstruation has been surrounded by taboos, myths, and restrictions that reinforce gender inequalities and curtail women's freedoms. The absence of scientific understanding about menstruation allowed these myths to flourish. Without accurate information, menstruation became a topic of speculation and secrecy, frequently passed down through generations as something shameful or forbidden."

The myths and misconceptions surrounding menstruation have deep roots in various cultures and societies, including religious beliefs, social norms, and historical misunderstandings about women's bodies. These myths have shaped how menstruation is perceived and often contributed to negative attitudes toward menstruating women.

In a society where patriarchy governs, women face countless restrictions. While it's impossible to ignore the inherent inequalities between the sexes, we must not let this blind us. It's important to recognize that gender is a social construct that perpetuates social inequality. Women have long endured various forms of inequality, often viewed as 'the second sex.' One significant issue revolves around menstrual taboos, which negatively affect women's physical, mental, and emotional health. The origins of these menstrual myths can be traced back to ancient texts such as the

Manusmriti and the Vedas. These revered scriptures, while highly esteemed, often fall victim to patriarchal interpretations, whether implicitly or explicitly. Despite these commonalities, we can still draw a list of comparisons between the two.

The laws of Manu or the Manusmriti were established by the sage Manu, a legendary figure considered the father of humanity and the ruler of the Earth. This text outlines a code of conduct and behaviour deemed 'the only appropriate' way for humanity. Unsurprisingly, these revered writings propagate patriarchal values and various forms of discrimination. Many Hindus adhere to these prescriptions without question, believing them to be the very words of God. It states:

41: For the wisdom, the energy, the strength, the sight, and the vitality of a man who approaches a woman covered with menstrual excretions, utterly perish.

42: If he avoids her, while she is in that condition, his wisdom, energy, strength, sight, and vitality will increase.

The Vedas are a compilation of hymns and other

ancient religious texts composed in India between approximately 1500 and 1000 BCE. They encompass mythological poems, guidelines for daily life, sacrifices, rituals, and codes of conduct. As the oldest texts foundational to Hinduism, the Vedas are regarded by Hindus as sacred, believed to have originated from God's mouth, despite the significant priestly bias inherent in them.

The Vedas do not contain any verses regarding the seclusion or restrictions placed on menstruating women. In fact, the 'Agnihotri yagna,' regarded as a significant ritual mentioned in the Vedas, is to be performed daily by the vaidiks (both men and women) without exception. If women were meant to be secluded and prohibited from worship during their menstrual cycles, how could they participate in this yagna? Thus, the Vedas do not impose restrictions on a woman's freedom or mobility due to a natural or mythical occurrence. However, drawing from the mythical story of Indra and Vritra, chapter five of the Vasishtha Dharmashastra introduces menstrual taboos, using them to reinforce women's subordinate status. These statements are both frivolous and provocative:

1. *Month by month, the menstrual flow absolves her of sins.*

2.

A woman is considered impure for three days and nights during her period.

3.

During her menstruation, she must not apply collyrium/ kajal to her eyes, anoint her body, bathe, sleep on a bed, sleep during the day, touch fire, make rope, clean her teeth, eat meat, gaze at the stars, or drink from a large vessel, joined hands, or a copper vessel.

I have spent a considerable amount of time researching this topic before offering this statement. One of the biggest confusions many Hindu women face is reconciling the idea that they are regarded as embodiments of Shakti, the divine feminine principle, while also being told they are impure during menstruation—unfit to perform Puja or, in some cases, even interact with their family.

To clarify these absurd notions let me explain the three body philosophy, The three bodies in Hinduism's three-body philosophy are:

1.

Sthūla śarīra: *The gross body, also referred to as the Annamaya Kosha, represents the physical form that experiences birth, aging, and death.*

2.

Sūkṣma śarīra: *The subtle body encompasses the*

mind and vital energies. It consists of three sheaths:

- ***Pranamaya Kosha:*** *The sheath of vitality or energy.*
- ***Manomaya Kosha:*** *The sheath of emotions.*
- ***Vijnanamaya Kosha:*** *The sheath of intellect and reasoning.*

3. ***Karaṇa śarīra:*** *The causal body, also known as the Anandamaya Kosha, represents the soul.*

The three-body philosophy is a fundamental principle in Indian philosophy and religion.

If try to understand only our Pranamaya kosha, our bodies contain five ***Pranas*** *or vital energies. These are:*

-

- ***Prana***: *energy that takes things in,*
- ***Apana***: *energy that expels things out,*
- ***Samana***: *energy that assimilates,*
- ***Vyana***: *energy that circulates and distributes, and*
- ***Udana***: *energy that expresses, particularly through speech.*

Any impediment to the flow of these Pranas causes imbalance and disease. For instance, an obstruction to Samana could lead to a metabolic or learning disorder. During religious rituals like Puja or Homa, there is a release of accumulated Prana.

Pranayama*—the practice of controlling Prana—helps balance the movement of these energies. More details on Prana and its functions can be found in Vedantic texts like Bodha Tattva, and are also mentioned in various other shastras.*

Menstruation is a time when ***Apana****, the energy responsible for expelling, is naturally predominant, and this serves a critical function. It allows for the outward flow of physical impurities, such as uterine* *tissue, and emotional release, like mood swings. Since religious practices like Puja aim to balance Prana, it's believed that engaging in them during menstruation, when Apana needs to dominate, may not be ideal.*

However, mental practices like ***Japa*** *(silent chanting) and* ***Manas Puja*** *(internal worship) are generally considered acceptable during menstruation, though this can vary depending on one's* ***Sampradaya*** *(spiritual tradition) or personal beliefs.*

This perspective explains why menstruation isn't about impurity, but rather about respecting the body's natural processes.

This book aims to explore the intricate analogy of the female reproductive system and menstruation while also unveiling captivating facts and folklore surrounding periods. It is designed to awaken curiosity and inspire both young and older generations to reflect on this natural process. By understanding the myths and stories associated with menstruation, we encourage both young girls and boys to inquire deeper and embrace the beauty of this sacred phenomenon— ***RUDHIRA****, the essence of feminine strength and vitality.*

Acknowledgements

Writing this book has been an enlightening and deeply personal journey, one that has required the guidance, support, and wisdom of many people.

First and foremost, I want to express my heartfelt gratitude to my family, particularly Anu Nadimpalli, for her unwavering support and encouragement throughout my journey. Your belief in my dream project and goals has been my anchor.

I extend my deepest thanks to Vedehi Sharma and her team, whose knowledge of menstrual health and folklore has been invaluable. Your insight and dedication to preserving and understanding cultural narratives around menstruation have shaped this book in ways I could not have imagined.

I am also incredibly grateful to the beautiful women from around the country who generously shared their stories, experiences, and perspectives on menstruation. Your openness and honesty about both traditional practices and modern experiences were vital to bringing authenticity to this work.

Lastly, to the readers of this book, thank you for joining me on this exploration of menstruation and the folklore surrounding it. It is through understanding and dialogue that we can break down taboos and embrace the richness of our shared histories.

With gratitude,
Dr Sanjhna Nayarr

Prologue

For centuries, menstruation has been surrounded by layers of myth, mystery, and silence. In every corner of the world, it is both a natural biological process and a powerful cultural symbol, woven into folklore, rituals, and societal taboos. Yet despite its universality, the subject of menstruation often remains hidden, tucked away in whispers and private conversations.

Growing up, I too was surrounded by the hushed tones of women discussing "that time of the month," often as though it were something to be ashamed of or concealed. I remember my mother passing on the same age-old practices and superstitions that had been taught to her, telling me to avoid certain foods, to rest, or to keep away from sacred spaces without giving me any explaination whatsoever. These instructions, passed down through generations, were rooted in a blend of care and caution, yet they were rarely questioned. For many women across cultures, menstruation has long been an experience steeped in tradition and secrecy.

But as I grew older and began to explore the stories of women from different parts of the world, I realized that menstruation holds much more than physical and emotional significance—it is a deeply ingrained cultural marker, one that has shaped identities, beliefs, and practices for millennia. From ancient myths to modern urban legends, menstruation has been portrayed as both a force of life and a source of fear, revered and yet stigmatized.

This book is an attempt to unravel some of those stories, to examine the folklore and traditions that have surrounded menstruation throughout history. It is a journey through time and across cultures, exploring the beliefs that have shaped how we understand our bodies and ourselves.

At its core, this is a conversation—a conversation that should have been happening more openly for generations. It's a reflection on how we, as a society, can move beyond the superstitions and silences that have kept menstruation in the shadows, towards a more open, informed, and respectful understanding of this vital aspect of life.

Whether you are reading this book out of curiosity, personal experience, or a desire to break the stigma surrounding menstruation, I hope it serves as a reminder that our stories—no matter how private or hidden—carry immense power. They connect us, challenge us, and offer us new ways of seeing the world.

Welcome to this journey.

Rudhira

The Scared Burnt Blood
A collection of folklores surrounding menstruation

श्रीगणेशायनमः।

ऊँअन्नादऽस्यापांतालभुवनमातरःस्वाहा।

ऊँवाग्देवतारुद्रस्याश्विनौमलेभताम्।

अनुप्रासात्समर्पयामि।

मातापार्वतीह्यसमनिप्रयुज्यतेच।

शुभंकरोति।

"Salutations to Lord Ganesha. May the mother bless me from the depths of the earth. May the divine word of the Ashwini Kumaras bless me. I offer this prayer and dedicate it to the auspicious Mother Parvati."

Introduction

In the ancient Hindu text Manusmriti (also known as the **Laws of Manu**), menstruation is viewed through a religious and cultural lens. The Manusmriti is one of the key legal and moral texts that shaped the societal norms and practices in ancient India. However, its teachings and views on menstruation reflect patriarchal values that were common at the time, and they have been heavily criticized in modern times.

Menstruation was often viewed through as a **mystery**, **taboo**, and **ritual contamination** across many cultures, including in societies influenced by religious or traditional beliefs. The way men viewed menstruation was largely shaped by these cultural, religious, and societal norms

In initial times, **mensus** (derived from the Latin word for "month") and **menstruation** were often understood in the context of their **biological**, **cultural**, and **religious** significance. It's interesting to know how menstruation was perceived in the olden days, touching on the meanings it carried in different aspects of life:

Biological Understanding:

- **Limited Medical Knowledge**: In ancient societies, menstruation was recognized as a natural, monthly event for women, but the scientific understanding of the process was limited. It was known that menstruation was linked to fertility and a woman's reproductive cycle, but the underlying physiology was not well understood. Early medical texts, like those from the Greeks and Romans, associated menstruation with **purging** the body of excess blood or "humors." This idea of menstruation as a form of **bodily cleansing** persisted for centuries.
- **Sign of Womanhood**: Menstruation marked a girl's transition into **womanhood**, signifying her ability to bear children. It was a **rite of passage**, and for many, it was linked to their reproductive role in society. Menstruation was seen as a sign of fertility and

sexual maturity.

Cultural and Social Views:

- **Ritual Impurity and Taboo**: In many ancient cultures, menstruation was closely associated with **ritual impurity**. Women were often restricted in their activities during menstruation, sometimes being isolated from society or prevented from participating in religious or household duties. This view was prevalent in societies such as ancient **Hindu**, **Jewish**, and **Christian** traditions. Menstruation was regarded as something to be managed carefully, and interaction with menstruating women could be considered defiling in a spiritual or ritualistic sense.
- **Secrecy and Silence**: Menstruation was often kept a **secret** and treated as a **taboo** subject. In many ancient societies, it was considered a private matter that wasn't openly discussed, especially amongst men. This secrecy further reinforced societal stigma and shame associated with menstruation.

Religious and Superstitious Beliefs:

- **Menstruation as Punishment**: In ancient religious texts, menstruation was sometimes described as a form of **divine punishment** or a consequence of original sin. For example, in the **Manusmriti** and certain interpretations of the **Bible**, menstruation was considered a curse on women for past sins. These interpretations contributed to the belief that menstruation was an impure or cursed process.
- **Supernatural Powers**: In some ancient cultures, menstruation was also associated with **supernatural** or **mystical** powers. While it was often viewed negatively, in some societies, menstrual blood was thought to have magical properties—either for good or evil. This duality added to the mystique surrounding menstruation, with men and women both holding menstruation

in a kind of fearful reverence.

Menstruation and fertility are deeply interconnected, with menstruation playing a crucial role in the reproductive cycle by preparing the body for potential pregnancy. Culturally, menstruation has been both revered and stigmatized, surrounded by folklore that ties it to fertility, life-giving powers, and taboos. In some cultures, menstrual blood was considered sacred and linked to fertility rituals, while in others, menstruation was seen as impure, leading to restrictions on women's activities. Modern understanding of menstruation focuses on education, challenging myths and taboos, and promoting awareness of reproductive health, empowering women with knowledge about their bodies and fertility.

- **Link to Fertility and Motherhood**: The onset of menstruation was directly linked to a woman's potential for **motherhood**. In agrarian and patriarchal societies, this gave menstruation an important place in social structures, where a woman's ability to bear children was highly valued. Failure to menstruate or irregular periods were often seen as problems related to fertility, sometimes even leading to **rituals or prayers** to restore the menstrual cycle.
- **Menstrual Blood and Life Force**: In some ancient societies, menstrual blood was seen as carrying a **life force** or essence, as it was linked to reproduction and fertility. Although it was often stigmatized as impure, it was also respected for its connection to the continuation of life.

Menstruation as a Social Divider:

- **Isolation and Exclusion**: In many cultures, menstruating women were **excluded** from daily activities, social gatherings, or religious ceremonies. For instance, in **ancient Hinduism**, menstruating women were not allowed to enter temples or kitchens. Similarly, in **ancient Judaism**, women were considered impure during their menstruation and had to undergo a purification ritual afterward. This separation reflected the societal view that menstruation was something that needed to be managed away from the public eye.

- **Menstrual Huts and Special Quarters**: In some ancient cultures, women were sent to **menstrual huts** or **special quarters** during their periods. For example, in some indigenous cultures, menstruating women would gather in separate spaces, away from the community, until their period ended. While this practice could be seen as isolating, in some contexts, it was also a form of **rest** or **spiritual reflection** for women.

Symbolism of Time and Cycle:

- **Connection to Lunar Cycles**: In many ancient cultures, menstruation was linked to the **lunar cycle**. The regularity of a woman's monthly cycle was often compared to the phases of the moon, and menstrual cycles were thought to have a mystical connection to **nature** and **time**. This connection to natural cycles further deepened the mystical and symbolic understanding of menstruation in many societies.
- **Marker of Time**: Menstruation was often used as a marker of time, both in terms of a woman's life stages (puberty, fertility, and menopause) and in relation to the passing of months. This was particularly important in societies where a woman's reproductive potential was closely monitored.

Breaking the Silence:

In recent decades, more open conversations about menstruation and fertility have emerged, challenging long-held myths and taboos. With greater awareness of reproductive health and women's rights, discussions about menstruation are moving away from the realm of superstition and stigma and toward education and empowerment.

Health campaigns and educational programs are helping to demystify menstruation and fertility, ensuring that women have access to accurate information about their reproductive health. This also extends to the intersection of menstruation and mental health, as menstrual cycles can be influenced by stress, diet, and lifestyle, all of which play a role in overall fertility.

The connection between menstruation and fertility is both biological and deeply cultural. On a physiological level, menstruation is an essential part of the reproductive process, indicating fertility and the potential for new life. Culturally, it has been revered, misunderstood, and mythologized throughout history.

By understanding both the science and the stories that surround menstruation, we can reclaim the narrative, breaking down taboos and embracing this vital aspect of womanhood with knowledge and respect.

Manusmriti 5.66

Sanskrit:

मासकिंतुरजोयस्यादारुणरंजसास्मृतम्।
तच्चापपिापकर्माण्याःपूर्ूवदोषान्नविर्ततो॥

"The monthly flow of blood, considered highly impure, is believed to be the result of sinful actions committed in previous lives."

CHAPTER ONE

REDISCOVERING THE WISDOM OF MENSTRUAL CYCLES

In India today, many women and girls are taught that menstruation is something impure, inconvenient, and burdensome—a fate to endure in silence. Meanwhile, in the West, advances in medicine have led to the creation of pills designed to stop menstruation altogether. However, ancient traditions held menstruation in high regard, recognizing it as a sacred and powerful process. Women were believed to possess unique energies during this time—energies that could either nurture life (leading to the reverence of women) or be seen as too potent (leading to the isolation of menstruating women). This duality speaks to the complex beauty of menstruation. To truly understand its significance, we must explore how menstrual cycles are intricately connected to lunar cycles and the unique transformations each phase brings.

Moon and Menstrual Cycle

For someone encountering this idea for the first time, it may seem strange to think that the Moon could influence what happens in our bodies! Did you know that both the menstrual cycle and the lunar cycle last approximately 28 days, and that women in ancient times reportedly menstruated simultaneously with the new moon?

Tracking your menstrual period in alignment with the Moon is one of the oldest methods of creating menstrual calendars. In fact, it is believed that the earliest calendars were developed based on women's recordings of their menstrual cycles and the lunar phases.

Long ago, before the advent of electricity and the shift to indoor living, women's menstrual cycles were deeply influenced by the natural light of the Moon. This idea suggests that moonlight served as a crucial synchronizing signal, known scientifically as a "zeitgeber," for regulating menstrual cycles—a connection that many of us have lost in today's world. Research from institutions such as Harvard University, the US Air Force, and the University of California, San Diego Sleep Center has shown that exposure to certain levels of artificial light during sleep can lead to more regular menstrual cycles in women.

Significance of each phase in the cycle

A woman's body undergoes four distinct stages during a menstrual cycle, mirroring the four seasons we experience each year. I found this comparison intriguing and could relate to much of the information, even though I had never actively recognized these changes happening within my body.

Week 1: Menstruation (Days 1-7) – This phase begins with the first day of bleeding, ideally coinciding with a new moon. Within hours of starting your period, your estrogen levels gradually begin to rise, marking a shift from the heaviness or PMS symptoms experienced in the days prior. This phase is viewed as a time for cleansing, allowing for the release of negative thoughts and emotions. Many women, myself included, have observed a strong urge to declutter our homes and clear out our closets during the first few days of our periods. This natural biological cleansing is mirrored by a psychological release as well.

This is a time when women often feel the need to retreat inward, embracing silence and contemplation. The rituals associated with seclusion during menstruation were, in part, designed to facilitate this introspective process.

Week 2: Pre-Ovulation (Days 7-14) – Following your period, this phase is when many women feel their most energized. The gradual rise in estrogen enhances serotonin levels in the brain, leading to increased energy, enthusiasm, and an overall uplifting mood. This period is ideal for launching new projects or engaging in creative endeavours.

Week 3: Ovulation (Days 14–21) – This phase marks ovulation, a time when women often appear more physically attractive and feel a heightened attraction to others. It's an important moment in our cycle for connecting with people and enjoying the outside world. However, it can also bring feelings of vulnerability, so it's crucial to remain grounded and mindful of our actions during this time.

Week 4: Pre-Menstruation (Days 21–28) – After ovulation, you'll notice the effects of declining estrogen and testosterone levels, alongside a rise in progesterone. Progesterone represents the 'ebb' in contrast to estrogen's 'flow,' prompting a desire to turn inward, much like the waning moon. Research indicates that during weeks 3 and 4 of your cycle, there is increased activity in the right hemisphere of the brain, which is linked to intuitive insights. Trust your intuition, but pay particularly close attention to it during the second half of your cycle!

Premenstrual Syndrome (PMS)

Many girls and women experience aches, pains, and mood swings in the days leading up to their periods. Here are some intriguing explanations found across various websites:

The premenstrual phase (week 4) encompasses the final days before the start of a new cycle. During this time, progesterone levels continue to rise until they, along with estrogen and testosterone, drop significantly at the end of this phase. If you ignore the natural urge to slow down and turn inward, feelings of resentment, frustration, and anger may begin to manifest.

The crankiness, impatience, or irritability commonly associated with Premenstrual Syndrome in the last two weeks of our cycle often stems from not aligning with what our bodies truly need.

Instead of embracing the natural urge to slow down, withdraw from the busyness of the outside world, and focus on self-care, we might find ourselves overwhelmed by the demands of others.

The premenstrual phase is, therefore, a period when we can tap into our inner magic—our capacity to identify and transform the more challenging and painful aspects of our lives. During this time, we naturally become more attuned to what truly matters to us. We may find ourselves more prone to tears, but these emotions are always connected to something significant in our lives.

The Moon influences all water on Earth, impacting every living being—humans, plants, animals, and fungi—since we are all primarily made up of water.

Women are a reflection of the Moon, embodying its phases and natural cycles. A symbol of femininity, mystery, renewal, and transitions. Since ancient times, the Greek and Latin languages have woven lunar imagery into our words. Just as the Moon moves through its cyclical phases, women experience their own monthly rhythms.

A few days before a woman's period starts, the production of the hormone progesterone stops, and the low levels of this hormone trigger menstrual bleeding. She explains that for menstruation to align with the full moon, the progesterone-producing structure would need to receive a signal ahead of the full moon.

Just as the Moon has its monthly cycles, women experience their own rhythmic phases. The phase of the Moon during which a woman bleeds reflects different intentions.

White Moon Cycle

When you bleed with the New Moon and ovulate with the Full Moon, you are in harmony with the Earth's natural rhythms. This is the time to plant seeds during the Full Moon, when both you and the Earth are at your most fertile. Your archetype during this phase is the mother, embodying nurturing qualities.

It's the best time to align yourself with the following thoughts:

- Are you wanting children?

- Do you take on the role of a mother in your relationships?
- Are you growing or nurturing a business of your own?
- What idea-babies are you wanting to manifest?

Pink Moon Cycle

When you bleed with the Waxing Moon and ovulate with the Waning Moon, you are undergoing a transition towards something greater and more luminous. This phase embodies the Maiden archetype—the enthusiastic go-getter within you, representing the young girl who aspires to become a free woman.

Best phase for the following:

- Are you in a phase of self-discovery?
- Who am I? Who will I become?
- What is my purpose to fulfill here in this phase of life?
- What risks are you willing to take to achieve this brighter future?
- What will make you feel more free?

Red Moon Cycle

If you bleed with the Full Moon and ovulate with the New Moon, indicating that you are here to showcase your talents and share your wisdom and gifts. This phase aligns with the Wise Woman archetype, embodying the healer, magic-maker, and keeper of wisdom. Additionally, she represents the enchantress and seductress, as her sexuality is not only used for procreation but also serves to empower other women and their communities.

Try considering the following during this cycle:

- Do you desire self-exploration & self-expression?
- Are you feeling finished with your mother role and turning your energy inward, of using your self-awareness to help heal the world?

Purple Moon Cycle

When you bleed with the Waning Moon and ovulate with the Waxing Moon, you are in a state of transition. You may feel a longing to reconnect with your true self, engaging in self-discovery and shedding old patterns to embrace a new identity. This phase embodies the Enchantress archetype, characterized by inner strength, spirituality, and fierce energy.

- Are you contemplating a career change?
- Do you seek deeper meaning in your work or personal life?
- Are you experiencing a sexual awakening, wanting to learn more about yourself and redefine your sensuality?
- Do you feel a pull inward, withdrawing from the outside world?

This information applies to anyone with a monthly cycle, regardless of whether you identify as a woman. The archetypes mentioned are fictional characters that represent different aspects of ourselves that we can relate to. Feel free to envision a character that resonates with you more, as long as they embody similar qualities!

For instance, the Wise Woman can take the form of a different Sage or Wise Elder, while the mother archetype could represent someone you see as nurturing and creative.

Always remember that you are part of nature. You are connected to all the elements around you and serve as a bridge between the Sky and the Earth. Pay attention to the shifts, transitions, and natural energies that flow both within you and in the world around you.

Menstruation and Fertility:

Menstruation and fertility are deeply interconnected, with menstruation playing a crucial role in the reproductive cycle by preparing the body for potential pregnancy. Culturally, menstruation has been both revered and stigmatized, surrounded by folklore that ties it to fertility, life-giving powers, and taboos. In some cultures, menstrual blood was considered sacred and linked to fertility rituals, while in others, menstruation was seen as impure, leading to restrictions on women's activities. Modern understanding of menstruation focuses on education, challenging myths and taboos, and promoting awareness of reproductive health, empowering women with knowledge about their bodies and fertility.

- **Link to Fertility and Motherhood**: The onset of menstruation was directly linked to a woman's potential for **motherhood**. In agrarian and patriarchal societies, this gave menstruation an important place in social structures, where a woman's ability to bear children was highly valued. Failure to menstruate or irregular periods were often seen as problems related to fertility, sometimes even leading to **rituals or prayers** to restore the menstrual cycle.
- **Menstrual Blood and Life Force**: In some ancient societies, menstrual blood was seen as carrying a **life force** or essence, as it was linked to reproduction and fertility. Although it was often stigmatized as impure, it was also respected for its connection to the continuation of life.

Menstruation as a Social Divider:

- **Isolation and Exclusion**: In many cultures, menstruating women were **excluded** from daily activities, social gatherings, or religious ceremonies. For instance, in **ancient Hinduism**, menstruating women were not allowed to enter temples or kitchens. Similarly, in **ancient Judaism**, women were considered impure during their menstruation and had to undergo a purification ritual afterward. This separation reflected the societal view that menstruation was something that needed to be managed away from the public eye.
- **Menstrual Huts and Special Quarters**: In some ancient cultures, women were sent to **menstrual huts** or **special quarters** during their periods. For example, in some indigenous cultures, menstruating women would gather in separate spaces,

away from the community, until their period ended. While this practice could be seen as isolating, in some contexts, it was also a form of **rest** or **spiritual reflection** for women.

Symbolism of Time and Cycle:

- **Connection to Lunar Cycles**: In many ancient cultures, menstruation was linked to the **lunar cycle**. The regularity of a woman's monthly cycle was often compared to the phases of the moon, and menstrual cycles were thought to have a mystical connection to **nature** and **time**. This connection to natural cycles further deepened the mystical and symbolic understanding of menstruation in many societies.
- **Marker of Time**: Menstruation was often used as a marker of time, both in terms of a woman's life stages (puberty, fertility, and menopause) and in relation to the passing of months. This was particularly important in societies where a woman's reproductive potential was closely monitored.

CHAPTER TWO

THE CURSE OF MENSTRUATION

Manusmriti 4.206

Sanskrit:

तस्याःस्पर्शणेभोजनंतदर्थदंत्तां

आश्रतियंत्रास्यत्यस्यस्नास्वयम्॥

Translation:

"By the touch of a menstruating woman, or by the food given by her, or by sitting in her presence, a man's spiritual vitality is destroyed."

Menstruation in the Manusmriti:

According to the Manusmriti, menstruation is seen as a form of **impurity** or a time of **ritual uncleanliness** for women. This concept is based on religious beliefs of pollution, which were a significant part of ancient Hindu customs. The above verse for example refers to the notion that being in the presence of a menstruating woman was considered impure, influencing the mindset that led to menstrual taboos.

Impurity and Sin: The Manusmriti claims that menstruation is a result of a woman's guilt or a form of punishment. It connects menstruation to a mythological sin, often believed to be the fault of women.

For example, in one verse (Manusmriti 5.66), it is stated that menstruation was a consequence of women accepting the guilt of killing a Brahmin (a priest or scholar), and thus, they must bear this mark every month.

1. **Restrictions During Menstruation:** The Manusmriti imposes several restrictions on women during their periods:

    - Women are often advised to refrain from participating in religious rituals or entering temples during menstruation.
    - They are not to touch or engage with certain household objects or family members, particularly those involved in religious ceremonies.
    - Specific dietary restrictions and isolation practices were sometimes enforced, requiring women to stay away from the household during their menstruation.

2. **Purification Rituals:** The Manusmriti suggests that after menstruation, women must undergo purification rituals before they can return to regular activities. This reflects the belief that menstruation is a form of bodily impurity that needs to be cleansed.

Context and Modern Reinterpretation:

- **Cultural Influence:** The Manusmriti heavily influenced societal views on menstruation in India for centuries, and many of its restrictive practices were followed in traditional Hindu households. However, modern interpretations of Hinduism and societal reforms have challenged these ideas, advocating for more positive and empowering views of menstruation.
- **Criticism:** Modern scholars, feminists, and activists criticize the Manusmriti for perpetuating patriarchal norms and gender discrimination. The idea that menstruation is a "punishment" or a "mark of sin" is seen as outdated, and modern efforts focus on destigmatizing menstruation and recognizing it as a natural biological process.
- **Change Over Time:** Many Hindu reform movements have emerged, rejecting the Manusmriti's views on menstruation and encouraging open discussions about menstrual health, hygiene,

and dignity for women. These movements emphasize the importance of understanding menstruation in a scientific, rather than superstitious, way.

Let me share a story which my grandmother used to tell me as to why women got their periods, though she did not have any basis for the same, however she strongly believed in the story.

In the olden times, when the world was still young, the balance between the divine, human, and natural worlds was carefully maintained. Among the deities, there was a revered Brahmin named **Vashishta**, known for his immense wisdom and profound knowledge of the Vedas. He was respected by all and had a close bond with the celestial beings.

One day, a powerful **Asura** (demon) named **Kumbhakarna** sought revenge against the Brahmins for an ancient slight. Envious of their knowledge and connection to the divine, he devised a plan to disrupt the harmony of the worlds. Kumbhakarna approached Vashishta, pretending to seek counsel, but secretly plotted to kill him. He tricked the Brahmin into a secluded place, where he unleashed his fury and struck down the sage.

The heavens trembled as the news of Vashishta's demise spread. The **Devas** (gods) were horrified by this heinous act. They convened in the celestial realm to discuss the dire consequences of Kumbhakarna's actions. After much deliberation, they decided that a punishment was necessary to restore balance and uphold the sanctity of life.

The goddess **Shakti**, representing feminine power, was summoned. She expressed deep sorrow for the Brahmin's death and determined that women would carry a burden as a reminder of the grave sin committed by Kumbhakarna. Thus, she decreed that every month, all women would experience menstruation, symbolizing both purification and the cyclical nature of life.

The Devas declared, "Let the blood that flows during this time serve as a reminder of the need to honor all life, to respect the sacredness of knowledge, and to maintain the balance of the universe." They also emphasized that menstruation was not a curse but a mark of strength and resilience, connecting women to the divine feminine energy and the cycles of nature.

As the first menstruation began, women learned to embrace this new aspect of their identity. They understood that their cycles were a reflection of the earth's rhythms, embodying fertility, creation, and destruction. It became a time of reflection, rituals, and a deep connection to their own bodies and the universe.

The story of Vashishta served as a cautionary tale for humanity, reminding everyone of the importance of respect, knowledge, and the delicate balance of life. Women, with their monthly cycles, became powerful vessels of life, carrying the lessons of the past while forging new paths for the future.

This tale underscores theme of respect for knowledge and life, the significance of feminine strength, and the cyclical nature of existence. It reflects the complex interplay between myth, culture, and the understanding of menstruation in ancient times.

According to a legend mentioned in the Rig Veda, Indra's nemesis was an Asura named Vṛttrasura, who also happened to be a Brahmin. (Some modern interpretations view this as a symbolic representation of the ongoing social conflict between the Kshatriyas, represented by Indra, and the Brahmins, represented by Vṛttrasura.)

After Indra defeated Vṛtra, who had stolen the gods' cows and hidden them in a cave, he was informed by Vishnu that he was now guilty of Brahminicide. To redeem himself and restore his position as the king of gods, as well as to regain his duties of providing rain to the earth, Indra had to distribute his guilt among the most virtuous creations of the gods.

Indra then approached three of the most virtuous creations and asked them to accept a portion of his guilt:

- **Earth** agreed, on the condition that she would never be fully depleted by being dug into. Indra granted her the boon that her cracks and hollows would eventually fill up. This is why sacred spaces are never created in natural hollows.

- **Trees** accepted on the condition that they would never be harmed by pruning. Indra blessed them with the ability to flourish even after being cut. This is why some trees exude sap when pruned, and these trees are not used in sacred rituals (Yajñas).
- **Women**, who are considered perpetually pure, accepted a portion of the guilt, resulting in their monthly menstruation, which symbolizes renewal and fertility through a few days of "impurity." Indra blessed women with fertility after their cycles, and also with the ability to experience sexual pleasure throughout much of pregnancy and even multiple orgasms.

Some versions of the story, like those in the **Taittiriya Samhita 2:5:1 (Krishna Yajur Veda)**, also include the **oceans**. Originally tranquil, the ocean took on periodic waves and turbulence. In Hindu tradition, oceans are often seen as "impure," and Brahmins who cross the ocean were believed to lose their caste status.

This myth has inspired various interpretations:

- Neo-Marxists may interpret it as evidence of the patriarchy's justification for controlling women.
- **Pauranikas** might consider it a historical truth that should be accepted as such.
- **Mīmāmsakas**, view it as a myth that explains natural phenomena—similar to the stork myth for explaining where babies come from—something that can be enjoyed in storytelling but not taken as literal fact.
- **Yajñikis** interpret it as a basis for their theory of ritual impurity.
- **Vedāntins** see the myth as an allegory for the nature of reality. Vṛtra represents ignorance (*Avidya*), while Indra, the spiritual seeker, wields the diamond thunderbolt (*vajra*) to destroy ignorance and liberate wisdom. The seven cows symbolize the light of wisdom concealed by delusive identities, and Indra's battle represents the struggle between knowledge and

ignorance.

In essence, the myth explains four natural phenomena through literary devices used in a pre-scientific age to entertain and provide insight into the nature of the world.

CHAPTER THREE

MENARCHE

Manusmriti 5.85
Sanskrit:
नरजस्वलायाःस्त्रयिाःस्पर्शंस्नात्वाऽन्यदाप्नोति।
ततःशुद्धरि्यस्याश्चतुर्थेऽहनि॥
Translation:
"A menstruating woman must not participate in religious or household duties, and after her period ends, she must undergo a purification process."

For many young girls, getting their first period, known as **menarche**, can be both exciting and nerve-wracking, especially if they are unfamiliar with what to expect. It can bring physical changes like cramps, bloating, and mood swings, as well as emotional shifts due to hormonal fluctuations. These changes can often be confusing for girls and sometimes overwhelming without proper guidance or education.

Menarche, though a term unfamiliar to many, is a significant milestone in every female's life. It symbolizes the transition from girlhood to womanhood and marks the onset of menstruation. This complex physiological event not only signals the start of a female's reproductive journey but also plays a crucial role in reflecting her overall health and well-being. Understanding its biological, emotional, cultural, and educational sides can help girls feel empowered and develop a healthy, positive view of menstruation and womanhood.

MENSTRUATION.

Thinking of which lets dive deep into the meaning of Menstruation.

Menstruation is a natural biological process that typically begins in girls during puberty, marking the start of their reproductive years. It occurs when the uterus sheds its lining, and this results in bleeding from the vagina, typically lasting between 3 to 7 days each month. The menstrual cycle, which is usually about 28 days long but can vary, is regulated by hormones such as estrogen and progesterone.

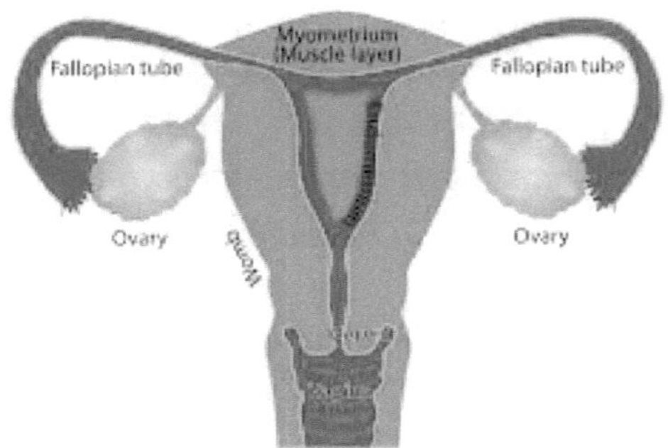

I understand anybody looking at this figure will be confused just like how they feel looking at it in our school textbooks. For all the people who want to understand a female reproductive system, all the clear explanation is given below. So just read on!!

The experience of a girl getting her first period, or **menarche**, is a significant milestone, both physically and emotionally. For many girls, it symbolizes the transition from childhood to adolescence. While some may feel excited, others might experience fear, confusion, or embarrassment, especially if they are unprepared or if the subject of menstruation hasn't been openly discussed with them beforehand.

What to Expect with the First Period:

1. **Timing:** Most girls experience their first period between the ages of 9 and 16, with the average being around 12. However, the age of menarche can vary depending on genetics, nutrition, and overall health. The menstrual cycle, typically lasting 28 days, is divided into several phases. The follicular phase starts on the first day of menstruation and continues until ovulation, around day 14. During this phase, FSH and LH stimulate the growth and maturation of ovarian follicles. At the end of the follicular phase, the mature follicle releases an egg, a process known as ovulation. After ovulation, the luteal phase begins and lasts until the next menstrual period. During this phase, the ruptured follicle forms the corpus luteum, which produces progesterone to sustain the endometrium in preparation for pregnancy. If fertilization does not occur, the corpus luteum breaks down, leading to menstruation.

1. **Physical Symptoms:**

    - **Spotting or light bleeding**: The first period may start with light spotting before becoming heavier, and it can be irregular at first.
    - **Cramps**: Some girls may experience mild cramps or discomfort in the lower abdomen.
    - **Bodily changes**: Menstruation is often preceded by other signs of puberty like breast development, hair growth in new areas, and mood swings.
    - **Discharge**: A whitish vaginal discharge may appear a few months or even years before the first period, which is a normal sign of the body preparing for menstruation.

3. **Emotional Reactions:**

    - **Anxiety or confusion**: Without prior knowledge, the sight of blood may cause panic or fear.

- **Excitement:** Some girls may feel proud or excited as this marks a step toward adulthood.
- **Embarrassment:** Especially in cases where the first period happens at school or in public, some girls might feel ashamed or self-conscious.

4. **Menstrual Products:** The use of pads, tampons, or menstrual cups can be a new experience. It's important that girls know their options, as well as how to use and dispose off them properly. Teaching girls to keep these items in their backpacks and to expect occasional irregular cycles can help them feel more prepared.

Emotional and Social Aspects:

1. **Family Support:** A mother, older sister, or female guardian often plays a key role in preparing a young girl for her first period. Open communication about menstruation can reduce fear and normalize the experience. Parents may find it helpful to create a supportive and shame-free environment by sharing personal stories or offering practical tips.
2. **School and Peer Influence:** Since periods can start at different ages, some girls may already know classmates who've experienced menarche, while others might feel like they're the only one. Peer support, or the lack of it, can significantly influence how a girl feels about menstruation.
3. **Cultural and Societal Perspectives:** In some cultures, menstruation is celebrated as a coming-of-age event, while in others, it may still be surrounded by silence or shame. A mother might have to navigate her own upbringing around periods to ensure that her daughter has a more positive experience.
4. **Educational Materials:** Today, there are more resources available to help girls understand menstruation, from books and pamphlets to videos and apps. Providing young girls with knowledge before their first period can help them feel confident

and informed.

CHAPTER FOUR

THE ULTIMATE CELEBRATION

Sanskrit:

मासमिासरिजःस्त्रीणांशुद्ध्यन्तक्ष्तिुकालतः।
रजस्वलासुनकर्तव्याधार्मकिैःसहसवंदिः॥

"Month after month, women become pure by the onset of their menstrual period. During their menstruation, the righteous should avoid contact or association with them."

The celebration of menarche across different traditions carries deep significance, reflecting various cultural, social, and emotional perspectives. Viewed as a crucial rite of passage, menarche signifies the transition from childhood to womanhood, with celebrations acknowledging the girl's growth and marking the beginning of her reproductive journey. These rituals often represent a community's cultural identity, showcasing the rich diversity of traditions and reinforcing shared values that foster a sense of belonging. Celebrating menarche can empower young girls by affirming their new roles within their families and society, allowing families to express pride and offer guidance during this significant transition. Many cultures also imbue these celebrations with spiritual meanings, emphasizing the sacred nature of womanhood and framing menstruation as a natural and divine process. Menarche celebrations foster community support, helping girls connect with peers and elders while creating a network of encouragement. Moreover, they serve to challenge societal taboos surrounding menstruation, promoting normalization and healthy attitudes toward women's health. These events often provide valuable educational moments, offering girls important information about reproductive health, self-care, and body positivity. Overall, the various traditions surrounding menarche celebrations highlight the importance of this milestone, encompassing cultural identity, empowerment, community support, and spiritual significance, while fostering resilience, confidence, and a strong sense of identity in young girls.

Celebration and Rituals

In many Hindu communities, menarche is celebrated with specific rituals that honour the girl's transition. These rituals can vary based on regional customs but generally include the following:

- **Bathing and Cleansing**: The girl is bathed and adorned in new clothes, symbolizing purification and rebirth.
- **Ceremonial Offerings**: Families may perform pujas (prayers) and make offerings to deities, acknowledging the spiritual significance of menstruation.
- **Gifts and Blessings**: The girl may receive gifts from family members, reinforcing her new status and the importance of her role in the family and society.

The perspectives surrounding menarche celebrations in various traditions underscore the significance of this milestone in a girl's life journey. These celebrations encompass cultural identity, empowerment, community support, and spiritual meaning, while also creating opportunities for education and breaking down taboos. Honouring menarche can play a crucial role in fostering positive attitudes toward menstruation and womanhood, enhancing resilience, confidence, and a strong sense of identity in young girls.

Here are some important perceptions related to these celebrations:

1. **Rite of Passage**
   Menarche is regarded as an essential rite of passage, signifying the shift from childhood to womanhood. Honouring this milestone acknowledges the girl's growth and the start of her reproductive journey, symbolizing her entrance into a new life phase.
2. **Cultural Identity**
   The customs and rituals associated with menarche celebrations often represent a community's cultural identity. These festivities can vary significantly between regions and communities, showcasing the rich diversity of traditions within society. They reinforce cultural values and practices, fostering a sense of belonging and continuity.
3. **Empowerment and Recognition**
   Celebrating menarche can empower young girls by affirming their new role and status within their families and society. This event allows families to express pride in their daughters and to offer support and guidance as they navigate this significant transition.
4. **Spiritual Significance**
   Many cultures imbue the celebration of menarche with spiritual meanings. These rituals typically include prayers, blessings, and offerings to deities, highlighting the sacred nature of womanhood and the belief that menstruation is a natural, divine process. This spiritual aspect can help demystify menstruation and frame it as a source of strength and fertility.
5. **Community and Support**
   Menarche celebrations often bring together family and community, fostering a sense of shared experience and support. This communal aspect helps girls connect with peers and elders, creating a network of encouragement as they transition into adulthood. It also provides a platform for sharing knowledge and experiences related to menstruation and womanhood.
6. **Breaking Taboos**
   The celebration of menarche can also challenge and dismantle

societal taboos surrounding menstruation. By openly discussing and honoring this natural process, families and communities can work toward normalizing menstruation, reducing stigma, and fostering healthy attitudes toward women's health.

7. **Education and Awareness**
   These celebrations often serve as educational moments for young girls, offering valuable information about menstruation, reproductive health, and self-care. They can help girls understand the physical and emotional changes they will encounter, promoting a positive body image and self-acceptance.

CHAPTER FIVE

THE SIGNIFICANCE OF RITUALS

Bhagavad Gita 9.26

पत्रंपुष्पंफलंतोयंयोमेभक्त्याप्रयच्छति।

तदहंभक्त्युपहृतमश्नामिप्रयतात्मनः

"if one offers to Me with devotion a leaf, a flower, a fruit, or even water, I delightfully partake of that item offered with love by My devotee in pure consciousness"

I was quite astonished to discover that menstruation rituals have remained remarkably similar around the world, from Native America to Europe, Africa, Australia, and Asia. Practices such as seclusion during menstruation and various taboos regarding food handling and entering sacred places have been documented globally. It seems that only in certain parts of Asia, like India, do we still observe many women adhering to these rituals today. This leads many of us to mistakenly believe that such "superstitions" are exclusive to developing countries like India. I have made an effort to research and gather insights from a wide range of sources to shed light on how these rituals may have originated. Here are some rituals, taboos, and thoughts about menstruation that I've managed to decode to some extent.

Menstruating women have to remain in seclusion until the period is over!!

Often, the justification provided in modern times is that menstruating women are considered impure, unclean, or dirty, and therefore should be kept apart.

Menstruating women were once believed to possess special powers during their menstrual cycles, which, if not handled properly, could potentially harm others. Additionally, practical concerns about predatory animals being attracted to the scent of blood in ancient times may have led to these women being housed in separate huts for the safety of the community. Since many ancestral women menstruated simultaneously with the new moon, these seclusion huts—often referred to as moon huts—were filled with women who shared their unique powers and engaged in sacred rituals for the benefit of the community. Those who emerged from these huts were respected for the visions and insights they gained during this time and often provided guidance to the community, such as advice on hunting locations.

What came as a terrifying to know was that this eventually prompted men to create similar rituals for adolescent boys to ensure they didn't feel excluded. As a result, ancient practices—still observed among some tribal communities—emerged, where young boys would beat themselves and cut their skin to induce bleeding, mimicking menstruation. They would also sting themselves with bees and ants to induce hallucinations, resembling the visions experienced by women during their menstrual cycles. Poor boys!

CHAPTER SIX

RITU KALA SAMSKARA

Bhagvad Gita Shloka:8

अहंसर्वस्यप्रभवोमत्तःसर्वंप्रवर्तते

"'I am the source of all spiritual and material and everything that exists emanates from Me."

In some south Indian communities, a girl's first period is celebrated with a coming-of-age ceremony called Ritusuddhi or Ritu Kala Samskara. The girl is given gifts and wears a traditional outfit called Langa Voni.

In certain cultures, a party or celebration is held to mark a girl's transition to womanhood. This event is akin to the quinceañera in Latin America, where a specific age signifies the transition rather than the onset of menarche. In Morocco, a similar celebration is organized for the girl. Menarche, the first menstruation, is celebrated in various ways across India, reflecting the country's rich cultural diversity.

Here are some notable celebrations in different regions:

Punjab

In Punjab, the celebration of a girl's first period is often marked by a ceremony known as **"Riti"** or **"Kanyadaan"**. Family and friends gather for a festive event that includes traditional music, dancing, and a feast. The girl is adorned in new clothes and jewellery, symbolizing her transition into womanhood. Often, blessings are sought from elders, and special prayers are recited.

Himachal Pradesh

In Himachal Pradesh, the celebration is called **"Chudakarana"**. This ceremony often takes place on the first day of menstruation and involves a puja (prayer ritual) performed by the girl's mother. Friends and family are invited to celebrate, and the girl is often gifted new clothes and jewellery. The occasion also includes feasting and blessings for health and prosperity.

Maharashtra

In Maharashtra, the first menstruation is celebrated with a ceremony called **"Valaikappu"** or **"Chudakarma"**. This is a joyous event that includes music and dance, where the girl is dressed in traditional attire. Friends and family members gather to offer blessings and gifts, emphasizing the importance of this life transition.

Tamil Nadu

In Tamil Nadu, the celebration is known as **"Mangalya Pooja"** or **"Poonal"**. The ceremony includes the girl undergoing a ritual bath, followed by the worship of deities. The family often prepares special foods, and gifts are given to the girl, symbolizing her new status. This celebration is marked by family gatherings and traditional customs.

Karnataka

In Karnataka, the first menstruation is celebrated with a ceremony called **"Chudakarma"** or **"Kanya Pooja."** The girl is treated with respect and pampered by family members. Special rituals are performed to invoke blessings, and she is adorned in new clothes. The occasion often includes a festive meal and the sharing of sweets with family and friends.

West Bengal

In West Bengal, the celebration of menarche is known as **"Nabanna"**. The girl's first period is celebrated with a puja, where she is dressed in traditional saree and adorned with jewellery. The family prepares a feast, and the girl is honoured as she steps into womanhood. It is a time of joy, often accompanied by singing and dancing.

Gujarat

In Gujarat, the celebration of a girl's first period is called **"Gharbha Sanskar"**. The girl undergoes a ritual bath, and family members perform pujas to bless her. The celebration includes traditional music, dance, and festive foods, highlighting the cultural significance of this milestone.

Andhra Pradesh and Telangana

In Andhra Pradesh and Telangana, the celebration is known as **"Chudakarma"** or **"Pellikuthuru"**. The girl's first period is celebrated with a special ceremony where she wears traditional attire and is honoured by family members. The occasion involves performing pujas, feasting, and sharing sweets with guest.

When a girl receives her first period, she is presented with a half saree and undergoes a ceremonial bathing in turmeric. Following this, the new half saree is draped on her, accompanied by a pooja to celebrate her transition into womanhood. Later in the day, her maternal uncle gifts her a saree, which is typically worn during the latter part of the day. The occasion is filled with a delightful array of food, gifts, and even monetary blessings.

As someone who grew up far from my hometown, I was unfamiliar with the ceremony. The thought that everyone—men and women alike—would know I was menstruating, and that it would be celebrated, felt completely foreign to me. Especially since I was still grappling with the awkwardness of puberty, often hiding sanitary pads deep in my pocket whenever I needed to change at school. Now, the entire family and beyond would be discussing my transition into 'womanhood.' The anticipation of embarrassment was overwhelming.

On the morning of the ceremony, I woke up to find myself draped in a flimsy cloth that barely covered my torso and upper legs while the men were shooed away to gather groceries and supplies. I was then made to sit on a small stool as my aunts, older sisters, and female cousins surrounded me. They began applying a thick mixture of turmeric, rose water, and other fragrant ingredients all over the exposed parts of my body—my face, neck, upper chest, arms, legs, and feet. I couldn't help but feel like a carrot cake smothered in cream cheese frosting.

I was left to bask in the gentle morning sun while everyone hurried to prepare for the ceremonial pooja and tidy up the house. In that moment, I couldn't help but reflect on the absurdity of it all, even as I appreciated how completely normal it felt to everyone around me. I understood that the origins of such ceremonies were rooted in patriarchy and outdated beliefs, yet the modern interpretation simply celebrates a girl! In Tamil culture, many milestones are celebrated with great fanfare—from the naming ceremony to the first morsel of food, and now this. In the grand scheme of things, it was just another reason to commemorate a natural part of life.

With a newfound sense of enthusiasm, my turmeric marination came to an end, and I was washed and ready to be dressed in my new half saree. I'll never forget standing in the middle of the room, clad in a blouse and petticoat, as my aunt draped the saree around me while everyone watched as if I were the eighth Wonder of the World. My hair was tied up and adorned with roses and jasmine, and I was decorated with a variety of jewelry. My cousins were frantically trying to decide which bindi would match my saree (we ultimately settled on two and crafted a delightful combination!). As cheesy as it may sound, I felt like a princess by the time I was ready, and the attention I received from everyone made me feel special. As an early teenager, being the center of attention wasn't typically my thing, but surrounded by family who meant well, I found comfort in their support.

Next came the ceremony with a priest and an altar of fire, following Hindu tradition, which seemed to pass in a blur (literally!). Just when I thought it was all over, the best part arrived: gifts and money! All my uncles, aunts, older cousins, and grandparents showered me with blessings and presents. With the grace of a rugby player on an ice hockey rink, I accepted it all with a grin. Afterward, I changed into a more comfortable outfit, enjoyed a big lunch.

This experience with a traditional ceremony completely transformed my understanding of menstruation. In today's world, menstruation is often cloaked in cultural taboos and traditions, so it was refreshing to participate in an experience that challenged my perceptions of my own period. While I was preoccupied with finding a sense of normalcy as my body underwent significant changes, and while I tried desperately to hide everything, here was a ceremony that joyfully celebrated this new milestone in my life.

CHAPTER SEVEN

MITHYA AND MENSTRUATION

Bhagvad Gita
Ch 2,shloka:63

क्रोधाद्भवतसिम्मोहः सम्मोहात्स्मृतविभि्रमः |स्मृतभि्रंशाद् बुद्धनिाशो
बुद्धनिाशात्प्रणश्यत

"From anger comes delusion and from delusion there is confusion of memory, and then there is loss of reason. From that, there is complete ruin."

Menstrual blood is often labelled as 'impure' or 'bad blood.'

However, all blood, including that of men, traces its origins back to menstrual blood. In ancient times, menstrual blood was regarded as highly powerful and potent, frequently used in various rituals and especially in the creation of magic potions. Even today, anything red used in ceremonies is thought to reflect the ancient practice of utilizing menstrual blood. One study suggests that the red mark on the foreheads of Hindu women originally represented menstrual blood. Likewise, the symbol of the Blood of Christ in Christianity is also believed to signify menstrual blood. Furthermore, the colour red, commonly associated with women's lipstick and cosmetics today—symbolizing seduction and power—has its roots in the use of menstrual blood by our ancestors to enhance their attractiveness.

Indian culture being one of the oldest civilizations with staunch beliefs, has somewhere failed to make the people stay on the facts behind all restrictions on women during their menstruation. The egoistic patriarchal society binged in their ideas of sabotaging women's freedom and purity under the pretext of our vedas.

Hinduism's characteristics of mensuration are wide-ranging as it is a stigma of purifying women are often separated from places of worship and any object possessing them.

Often, we hear, even today that girls and women who are having their periods cannot enter any temple.

There are specific rules for women during menstruation, which can be divided into two categories: those based on Vedic and Shastra traditions, and those rooted in Tantra, which often contradict Vedic practices. In Tantra, menstruation is seen as a significant event for achieving spiritual powers or *siddhis*. However, this knowledge is passed through a Guru-Disciple relationship and is not published publicly. I can share this wisdom, but only with sincere disciples.

Let's focus on logic and science rather than quoting texts or using jargon, which can easily be found online. What cannot be copied or pasted is the true understanding, the essence and rhythm of Vedas and Shastras, which requires a deep, subtle level of comprehension. Many may perceive contradictions in these texts, but these contradictions dissolve with deeper insight. Let me share something that can be understood at a basic level.

Menstruation, like defecation or urination, purifies the body internally but leaves a person *apavitra* (impure) externally, rendering them ineligible for Vedic rituals and worship. This state of impurity extends to menstruating women, postpartum women, and anyone who hasn't bathed after relieving themselves. There's also *ashauch* (impurity) related to birth and death, which varies according to local customs.

This state of impurity is washed away through ritual cleansing. Women after menstruation undergo an important bath called *Ritu Snan*, after which they are fully eligible to participate in Vedic rites.

Contrary to beliefs in other religions, like Islam, there is no intention in our scriptures to demean women. The reason for impurity during menstruation (typically three days) is that women are expelling unused eggs, filled with life force. Hormonal changes during this time, such as fluctuations in estrogen and progesterone, can cause mood swings or depressive tendencies, which vary depending on the woman's personality. However, some women can channel this energy towards spiritual growth and achieve higher realms of consciousness.

"Menstruating women should not enter temples or participate in religious ceremonies."

This particular taboo can be deeply upsetting for many religious women and young girls. The recurring question often is, "Am I so unclean during my period that even God wants me to stay away?"

Unfortunately, no one, not even the esteemed women who uphold this belief, has been able to provide a positive explanation for this restriction. After considerable research and exploration, I have discovered a few perspectives that suggest these guidelines are intended to protect women rather than isolate them.

One belief is that menstruating women are continually releasing energy from their bodies. Many religious chants are designed to harmonize the energies within us, but this can disrupt the natural energy loss that menstruating women experience, which helps prevent excessive energy buildup. Therefore, they are advised to refrain from participating in these practices to avoid interfering with their natural processes.

Another explanation I encountered is that menstruating women are more receptive to energies during this time, making them susceptible to absorbing both positive and negative influences. For this reason, they are encouraged to avoid crowds and large gatherings.

There is countless occult practices related to menstruation. Women have an advantage here, as the menstrual energy can be harnessed for spiritual or paranormal growth. When directed upwards, a woman can become *Urdhwaretas*—a master of channelling energy toward divine faculties. However, this power can also be misused, and like all occult practices, it carries karmic consequences.

The three days of menstruation serve as a natural cleansing process. Women are rejuvenated after this period, often feeling renewed and energized. The bath, *Ritu Snan*, helps clear away physical and metaphysical negativity. It is a time for women to rest, as engaging in household tasks during this time can cause further discomfort. This natural cycle of rest is actually a sign of vitality, not a form of degradation.

Because of these reasons, women in menstruation are not allowed to enter temples (with the exception of a few Tantric temples) or participate in Vedic rituals. This isn't a big issue—skipping three days of temple worship is not a major inconvenience, and it's aligned with the natural cycle of the body.

In our scriptures, women are regarded as equals to men. They are often described as more powerful, even surpassing their Rishi or God-husbands in wisdom. Great women from the Vedic period, such as Gargi, Maitreyi, and Arundhati, were highly respected for their intelligence and knowledge of the Shastras.

Shastras are unbiased, logical, and based on universal laws (*Ritam*). While men have numerous rituals and rules to follow, women have far fewer requirements. For instance, women can participate in Vedic worship without a *Janeu* (sacred thread), while men cannot. Women also have the option, not the obligation, to perform certain rituals, which are mandatory for men.

From a Tantric perspective, the rules around menstruation are different. During menstruation, a woman is seen as a powerful deity, representing the life-giving process of nature. Tantra has specific practices that can only be performed during this time, offering the opportunity for immense spiritual and occult achievements. While rare, these practices exist and are guarded by knowledgeable gurus.

In summary, the prohibitions around menstruation in temples are not designed to demean women, but to honor the natural cycle and provide rest. Temples do not check for menstruation, so it's often a matter of personal conscience. Respecting these traditions is not about inequality, but rather recognizing the significance of menstruation and the need for rest during this time.

Scriptures are not to blame for any perceived bias—understanding the deeper truth behind these rules reveals their utilitarian nature. If someone believes that entering a temple during menstruation is necessary for their sense of freedom or equality, it's likely a personal or collective ego issue, rather than a problem with the Vedic rules. Intelligent, unbiased individuals generally find no issue with taking rest during menstruation—it's a natural time for "me-time."

In my opinion, these ancient traditions carry significant messages for all of us, originating from a time when women were revered and seen as divine beings, with their wisdom cherished by the entire community. In contemporary discussions about the rising crimes against women, we often frame the conversation in terms of feminism or gender equality. However, we must remember that we live in a predominantly religious society, and many people do not resonate with the academic language of feminism. Perhaps it is through these stories that we can sow the seeds of change in both men and women, encouraging a shift in attitudes and treatment toward women.

CHAPTER EIGHT

ANCIENT CIVILIZATION AND MENSTRUAL FOLKLORE

Manusmriti
Verse 5.108
"अद्भिर्गात्राणिशुध्यन्तिमनःसत्येनशुध्यति।
विद्यातपोभ्याभूतात्माबुद्धिर्ज्ञानेनशुध्यति॥
"The limbs are purified by water; the mind is purified by truthfulness; the soul proper by learning and austerity; and cognition is purified by knowledge"

Across the globe, diverse cultural and religious beliefs and customs surrounding menstruation often concentrate stories about periods, gynaecological issues and taboos. Menstruation has been a fundamental aspect of human life for thousands of years, yet our understanding and societal views on it have changed significantly over time. This evolution, characterized by myths, misconceptions, and scientific progress, mirrors broader shifts in culture, medicine, and gender roles. Let's delve into the history of menstruation and examine how far we've come.

In numerous early societies, menstruation was cloaked in mystery and frequently linked to various myths and superstitions. The Ancient Greeks held the belief that menstruation served as a means for the body to eliminate excess blood, a concept grounded in the humoral theory of medicine, which posited that human health relied on the balance of bodily fluids, including blood. This belief continued to influence perceptions and treatments of menstruation well into the Middle Ages.

In contrast, the Romans attributed magical properties to menstrual blood. Pliny the Elder, a Roman author, noted in his work *Natural History* that menstrual blood could repel pests from crops, dull the sharpness of steel, and even induce madness in dogs. These beliefs highlight the complex emotions surrounding menstruation—both reverence and fear—mirroring the broader Roman perspective that intertwined natural phenomena with superstitious beliefs.

The Ancient Egyptians had their own interpretations of menstruation, perceiving it as a form of purification and believing in the medicinal properties of menstrual blood. Some ancient texts indicate that menstrual blood was utilized in potions or healing rituals, reflecting the intricate and often contradictory attitudes toward menstruation found in early cultures.

In Mesoamerican cultures, including the Maya and the Aztecs, menstruation was deeply connected to religious and cultural beliefs. The Aztecs viewed menstruation as a manifestation of the moon goddess's influence, regarding menstruating women as being temporarily under her protection. However, this belief also led to menstruating women being often barred from participating in certain religious ceremonies and daily activities, emphasizing the notion that menstruation was both a powerful and potentially perilous force.

Menstrual Taboos Across Cultures

Throughout history, menstrual taboos have been prevalent in many cultures, often leading to the stigmatization of menstruating women. In Hindu tradition, for instance, women are frequently excluded from daily activities and rituals during their menstrual cycles, based on the belief that menstruation renders them ritually impure. This notion continues to exist in some communities today, where menstruating women are still barred from entering temples or fulfilling religious duties.

Similarly, certain African and Indigenous cultures have employed menstrual huts to separate menstruating women from the rest of the community. Often referred to as "menstrual seclusion huts," these structures are typically situated on the outskirts of villages, symbolizing the perceived necessity of isolating menstruating women due to their "impurity." Although the specifics of these practices vary widely, they all serve to reinforce gender inequalities and perpetuate the idea that menstruation is something shameful or dangerous.

In Jewish tradition, the concept of **niddah** pertains to the state of ritual impurity associated with menstruation. During this time, women are traditionally required to abstain from sexual relations and certain religious practices until they undergo a ritual bath, known as a **mikvah**, at the end of their menstrual period. While contemporary interpretations and practices may differ, the idea of niddah has historically emphasized menstruation as a condition of impurity necessitating ritual cleansing.

In Indigenous Australian cultures, menstruation is sometimes viewed as a period of heightened spiritual power. However, this belief also leads to menstruating women being separated from the community and restricted from participating in certain activities. This complexity in attitudes toward menstruation illustrates a broader pattern across various cultures, where menstruation is simultaneously revered and feared.

Let me share few more elaborated narratives for each civilization, portraying their beliefs about menstruation through engaging folklores:

Ancient Hindu Civilization

In a small village nestled by the sacred river Ganga, a young girl named **Aditi** eagerly awaited her first period. The villagers whispered of the day when she would become a woman, but they also warned her of the rules that came with it. As the day approached, Aditi's mother, **Lakshmi**, spoke gently of the traditions: "When your time comes, you will enter the sacred space of womanhood, but you must respect the rituals of purity."

When Aditi finally felt the change within her, she was both excited and frightened. The village elder performed a puja (prayer) to authenticate her transition, marking the occasion with blessings and sweets. However, as she entered her first menstruation, Aditi was confined to a small room, separate from her family. She gazed out the window, watching her friends play, feeling the weight of the traditions. Yet, she also sensed a power within herself, knowing she was now connected to the cycles of life and the divine feminine energy.

Ancient Egyptian Civilization

In the heart of **Thebes**, the sun shone brightly on the bustling markets. **Nefertari**, a young woman in her early teens, was about to experience her first menstruation. Her grandmother, **Merit**, shared stories of the goddess **Isis**, who was revered for her wisdom and power. "Menstruation is a gift from the gods, Nefertari," she said. "It connects you to the life force."

One day, Nefertari felt a strange sensation. She rushed to her grandmother, who smiled knowingly. "Welcome to womanhood, my dear. Embrace this moment!" Nefertari learned to appreciate her body's rhythms, understanding that her menstrual blood was sacred. In her village, women gathered during their periods, sharing stories and creating bonds. It was a time of power, healing, and connection to the earth, reflecting the vitality of life itself.

Ancient Greek Civilization

In ancient Athens, a bright and curious girl named **Sophia** was captivated by the teachings of philosophers like **Hippocrates**. As she approached her first period, she overheard her mother discussing the mysteries of women's bodies. "Menstruation is a natural process," her mother said. "It purges the body of excess humors."

One fateful evening, Sophia felt the familiar signs. She was excited yet nervous about what it meant. That night, she gathered with her friends under the stars, sharing stories about their coming-of-age. Yet, as the moon rose high, some older women warned,

"Beware! Your blood can sour wine and bring bad luck!" These mixed messages filled Sophia with confusion. As she navigated her new reality, she learned to appreciate her body while understanding the tension between fear and respect that surrounded menstruation.

Ancient Roman Civilization

In ancient Rome, a spirited girl named **Clara** was on the cusp of womanhood. The marketplace buzzed with life as she ran through the streets, eager to explore the world. But her joy was tempered by the shadow of fear surrounding menstruation. The tales of menstruating women polluting gardens and rusting iron haunted her thoughts.

When Clara's first period arrived, her mother, **Livia**, took her aside. "My dear, you must understand the rituals of our people. While your blood is powerful, it also requires respect." Clara was confined to her room for several days, marked as a time of purification. But during her isolation, she discovered strength in her femininity and formed a bond with her blood, recognizing its connection to fertility and life. Through her challenges, Clara became a symbol of resilience, embracing the duality of her nature.

Ancient Jewish Civilization

In a small village in Judea, **Miriam** eagerly anticipated her first period, which marked her transition into womanhood. Her mother, **Hannah**, shared stories from the **Torah**, emphasizing the significance of being **niddah**—a state of ritual impurity during menstruation. "You will have a sacred duty, my daughter," Hannah explained, preparing Miriam for what lay ahead.

The day came when Miriam felt the change within her. Her heart raced with both excitement and anxiety. As she entered her room, her mother explained the purification rituals and the importance of the mikvah—a ritual bath that would cleanse her after her period. With time, Miriam learned to navigate her newfound status. She embraced the separation, understanding it as a spiritual journey. With each cycle, she found strength in her identity as a woman, connecting to her community and honouring the sacredness of life.

Ancient Chinese Civilization

In the serene landscapes of **ancient China**, **Mei Ling**, a curious young girl, lived by the principles of **Yin and Yang**. As she approached her first period, her grandmother, **Jin**, taught her about the balance of energies within her body. "Menstruation is the release of Yin, a time for reflection and rejuvenation," she explained.

When Mei Ling finally experienced her first menstruation, she felt a mix of emotions. Her family honored her transition with a small celebration, emphasizing the importance of maintaining harmony in her body. Mei Ling learned to respect the process, understanding that menstrual blood symbolized not just fertility but also the cyclical nature of life. During her periods, she engaged in quiet reflection and embraced the rhythm of the seasons, feeling empowered by her connection to nature and the world around her.

Native American Tribes

In the heart of the **Great Plains**, a young girl named **Wynona** awaited her first menstruation with a blend of excitement and trepidation. In her tribe, this rite of passage was celebrated with reverence. Her mother, **Ashi**, explained, "When you bleed for the first time, it's a sign that you have entered a sacred space. You will be powerful, and your connection to the earth will deepen."

When the day finally arrived, Wynona was guided to a special **menstrual hut**, a place where she could reflect and embrace her newfound identity. The other women shared stories of their own journeys, celebrating the energy and strength that came with womanhood. As Wynona emerged from her time in the hut, she felt a profound connection to her ancestors and the land. She understood her power and responsibility, vowing to honour the cycle of life and the strength of femininity.

Ancient Mesopotamian Civilization

In the bustling city of **Babylon**, a girl named **Inanna** anticipated her first period with a sense of wonder. The whispers of her elders spoke of the dual nature of menstruation—both a source of life and a marker of impurity. As she prepared for the transition, her mother, **Zara**, recounted the tales of the goddess **Inanna**, who represented fertility and love.

When Inanna's first menstruation arrived, she felt a mixture of pride and trepidation. Her family performed a ritual to honour her transition, acknowledging both the sacred and taboo aspects of menstruation. Inanna learned about the importance of ritual purity, the need for separation, and the power she held as a woman. With each cycle, she embraced her femininity and understood that her blood was a link to the divine, a connection to the cycle of life and the earth.

Through these stories, we can see how the beliefs surrounding menstruation in ancient civilizations shaped women's experiences and identities. While often intertwined with concepts of purity and taboo, they also offered avenues for empowerment and connection to the divine and the earth.

The Evolution of Medical Views on Menstruation

Even in the absence of scientific clarity, early efforts were made to explain menstruation through various medical theories. Medieval practitioners, such as Hildegard of Bingen—a Benedictine abbess and polymath—sought to document menstrual cycles and women's health. However, their interpretations were significantly shaped by the dominant religious and cultural beliefs of their era. For instance, Hildegard regarded menstruation as a natural occurrence but also believed it was connected to the spiritual and moral well-being of women.

In the Islamic world, scholars like Avicenna (Ibn Sina) made notable contributions to medical knowledge, particularly regarding menstruation. His 11th-century work, *The Canon of Medicine*, was an extensive medical text that included discussions on menstruation and women's health. Avicenna adopted a more scientific approach to menstruation, emphasizing its importance for female health and reproduction, even as his ideas remained influenced by the humoral theory prevalent in medieval medicine.

The Renaissance heralded a new era of scientific inquiry into the human body. Physicians started to investigate menstruation more methodically, shifting away from solely religious or superstitious interpretations. The advent of the printing press in the 15th century played a crucial role in disseminating medical knowledge, leading to a broader and more standardized understanding of menstruation.

During this time, the idea of 'menstrual blood' being distinct from other types of blood in the body began to be questioned. Physicians and scientists started to acknowledge menstruation as a normal physiological process, even though numerous myths and misconceptions continued to thrive. For instance, it was widely thought that menstruation was essential for a woman's health by purging excess blood, a belief that remained until the emergence of modern medical science.

However, as medical knowledge improved, views on menstruation started to change, but societal attitudes took longer to catch up. Menstrual taboos continued to exist in many cultures, even though the scientific community's increasing focus on female biology led to more accurate studies in later centuries. The Enlightenment period of the 17th and 18th centuries brought additional advancements in the understanding of menstruation. Scholars such as William Harvey, who discovered blood circulation, helped foster a more scientific perspective on the menstrual cycle. Nevertheless, societal attitudes toward menstruation largely remained negative, and women continued to experience stigma and discrimination related to their menstrual status.

CHAPTER NINE

MYTHOLOGICAL REVERENCE

Manusmriti

Verse 1.22

कर्मात्मनांचदेवानांसोऽसृजत्प्राणिनांप्रभुः।

साध्यानांचगणंसूक्ष्मंयज्ञंचैवसनातनम्॥२२॥

"For the sake of living beings intent upon action, he created the eternal sacrifice; as also the host of Gods and the subtile multitude of the lesser divinities, the Sādhyas."

Menstruation is viewed through various lenses across cultures, and in some places, it is celebrated and honoured as a natural and sacred aspect of womanhood. The worship of Shakti for menstruation is deeply rooted in the recognition of femininity, strength, and the natural cycles of life. This reverence serves to empower women, celebrate their unique experiences, and honour the sacredness of their bodies. By acknowledging menstruation as a significant aspect of womanhood, devotees can foster a deeper understanding of the divine feminine and its role in the world.

Shakti, representing divine feminine energy and power in Hinduism, is worshipped for menstruation due to several interconnected reasons that celebrate femininity, fertility, and the cycles of life. Shakti embodies the creative and nurturing aspects of the divine feminine. Menstruation, as a natural process, is often seen as a reflection of this energy, symbolizing the ability of women to create and sustain life. By worshipping Shakti, devotees acknowledge and honour this essential aspect of womanhood. Menstruation is inherently tied to the cycles of nature, mirroring the phases of the moon and the rhythms of the earth. Worshipping Shakti reinforces the understanding that menstruation is a natural and sacred process, integral to the cycle of life, growth, and regeneration. Shakti is often associated with nature, fertility, and the Earth, further emphasizing this connection. Shakti is not only a symbol of fertility but also of strength and power. Menstruation is viewed as a manifestation of a woman's inherent strength and resilience. Celebrating Shakti during menstruation acknowledges the power that women possess and their ability to endure physical and emotional challenges. Temples dedicated to various forms of the goddess often incorporate rituals that celebrate menstruation, recognizing it as a sacred and vital aspect of femininity. These practices can empower women and create a sense of community and support. In some traditions, menstruation is seen as a time of transformation and purification. Shakti's worship during this phase symbolizes the renewal of energy and life. The rituals associated with menstruation often emphasize cleansing, healing, and reconnecting with one's inner self, further underscoring the sacredness of this time. Worshipping Shakti in relation to menstruation can help challenge and break the taboos surrounding this natural process. By honouring the divine feminine during menstruation, communities can promote healthy attitudes and discussions about menstruation, reducing stigma and fostering acceptance.

Here are a few temples and sites around the world where menstruation is worshipped or recognized:

Kamakhya Temple, Assam, India

Located in the northeastern state of Assam, Kamakhya Temple is one of the most famous Shakti Peethas dedicated to the goddess Kamakhya. The Kamakhya Temple in Guwahati, Assam, is renowned for its association with a Goddess who experiences menstruation. Revered as an incarnation of Goddess Kali, who is herself a reincarnation of Goddess Parvati, Kamakhya Devi is said to bleed for three days. During this time, the temple remains closed, and pilgrims from across the country gather for the annual festival held on the grounds. It is believed that the Goddess menstruates each year during the monsoon season.

For the duration of these three days, devotees are advised against gardening, cooking, engaging in religious activities, or performing any veneration (puja). After this period, the temple is reopened with rituals that symbolize the renewal of fertility and life.

The Legend of Sati:
Sati, the daughter of King Daksha, married Lord Shiva against her father's wishes. During a grand yagna (sacrificial ceremony) hosted by Daksha, Sati was not invited. However, she went to the yagna, hoping to reconcile with her father. Unfortunately, Daksha insulted Shiva, leading to Sati's profound grief. Unable to bear the humiliation of her husband, Sati sacrificed herself in the fire of the yagna.

Shiva's Grief:
Distraught by the loss of Sati, Shiva performed the **Tandava**, a cosmic dance of destruction, which led to chaos in the universe. To restore balance, the gods pleaded with Shiva to calm down. In his grief, he carried Sati's charred body and wandered the universe, causing further disruption.

The Shakti Peethas:
To stop Shiva's destructive dance, Lord Vishnu intervened. He used his discus to cut Sati's body into 51 pieces, which fell across different parts of India. Each site where a piece landed became a **Shakti Peetha**, a sacred site dedicated to the goddess. The Kamakhya Temple marks the location where Sati's yoni (female reproductive organ) is believed to have fallen.

Significance of the Temple

- **Worship of the Goddess:**
  The Kamakhya Temple is unique because it doesn't have a traditional idol. Instead, it features a **yoni-shaped stone,**

symbolizing the goddess's feminine energy. The temple attracts devotees seeking blessings for fertility, health, and well-being.

- **Menstruation and the Goddess**:
  One of the most significant aspects of the Kamakhya Temple is the belief that the goddess undergoes her menstrual cycle. This phenomenon occurs during the **Ambubachi Mela**, a festival celebrated in June, when the temple is closed for three days. Devotees believe that during this time, the goddess is menstruating, symbolizing fertility and the natural cycles of life. After the three days, the temple is reopened with rituals that signify renewal and fertility.
- **Cultural Heritage**:
  The temple is not just a religious site but also a cultural hub, celebrating the unique traditions of the region. Pilgrims and tourists visit the temple to participate in various festivals, rituals, and ceremonies throughout the year.

The Kamakhya Temple stands as a testament to the rich tapestry of mythology, spirituality, and cultural identity in India. Its association with menstruation and the divine feminine emphasizes the significance of women's natural cycles and their connection to the goddess. This temple continues to be a vital center for worship, drawing countless devotees seeking blessings and a deeper connection to the divine.

The Menstruating Goddess, A Woman's Festival, Egypt

In ancient Egypt, goddess figures like Hathor and Isis were associated with femininity, fertility, and menstruation. While specific temples may not exist solely for menstruation, the reverence for these goddesses reflects the acknowledgment of women's cycles and their connection to nature and fertility.

The concept of "The Menstruating Goddess" in ancient Egyptian culture is rooted in the reverence for feminine cycles and the divine aspects associated with womanhood. While there may not be a specific festival exclusively dedicated to the menstruating goddess, several deities in ancient Egypt were associated with femininity, fertility, and the natural cycles of life. Here's an exploration of the story and significance surrounding this concept:

The Goddesses of Fertility and Womanhood

1. **Isis**:
   Isis was one of the most important goddesses in ancient Egypt, revered as the goddess of fertility, motherhood, and magic. She was often depicted as a nurturing figure, associated with the protection and sustenance of women and children. Isis's connection to motherhood and fertility links her to the cycles of women, including menstruation, as an integral part of life and creation.
2. **Hathor**:
   Hathor, another significant goddess, was associated with love, beauty, music, and fertility. She was often depicted as a cow or a woman with cow horns, symbolizing nourishment and maternal care. Hathor's connection to fertility and the female body resonates with the natural cycles, celebrating the power and sanctity of womanhood.

The Festival of the Menstruating Goddess

While there may not be a specific festival solely focused on the menstruating goddess, the ancient Egyptians celebrated various festivals that honored the feminine aspects of their deities and the cycles of life:

1. **Celebration of Fertility**:
   Festivals in honour of goddesses like Isis and Hathor often involved rituals celebrating fertility, motherhood, and the cycles of nature. These festivities acknowledged the natural processes of life, including menstruation, as sacred and vital to the continuity of existence.
2. **Rituals and Symbolism**:
   Rituals associated with these festivals could involve offerings, prayers, and communal gatherings, emphasizing the importance

of women's roles in society. The menstrual cycle was seen as a connection to the divine, with women viewed as sacred vessels of life.

Significance in Ancient Egyptian Society

1. **Cultural Reverence**:
   The reverence for the menstruating goddess reflects a broader cultural recognition of the importance of femininity and fertility. Women were celebrated as essential contributors to society, and their natural cycles were viewed as vital to the community's well-being.
2. **Spiritual Connections**:
   The belief in goddesses associated with menstruation highlights the spiritual connection between women and the divine. Menstruation was seen as a natural process that linked women to the cycles of nature, reinforcing the idea of womanhood as sacred.
3. **Breaking Taboos**:
   By celebrating the menstrual cycle through the lens of divine femininity, ancient Egyptians may have worked to normalize and honor this natural process, reducing stigma and acknowledging its significance in the cycle of life.

The story of "The Menstruating Goddess" in ancient Egypt emphasizes the reverence for feminine cycles and the natural processes of life. Through the worship of goddesses like Isis and Hathor, ancient Egyptians celebrated the sanctity of womanhood, fertility, and the menstrual cycle as integral aspects of existence. These cultural beliefs fostered a deep appreciation for the divine feminine and its role in nurturing life, highlighting the importance of women in society.

Chengannur Mahadeva Temple in Kerala.

The **Chengannur Mahadeva Temple** in Kerala's Alappuzha district is notable not only for its architectural beauty and historical significance but also for its unique connections to menstruation and feminine divinity. The Chengannur Mahadeva Temple, situated in Chengannur, Kerala, is dedicated to Lord Shiva and Goddess Bhadrakali, an incarnation of Sati or Parvati and the deity of the state. This temple is renowned across the country for its unique menstruation festival, during which the temple remains closed for three days.

Devotees believe that the Goddess experiences irregular menstruation. According to a mythological story, people believe that Goddess Parvati came here from the Himalayas after marrying Lord Shiva. She had periods here, which went for about 28 days. Another story revolves around Sage Agastya, who, for some reason, was unable to witness the wedding of Lord Shiva and Goddess Parvati. In response, the couple decided to visit the sage. It is said that Goddess Parvati started her menstrual cycle during their journey to meet Agastya. Consequently, she waited for 28 days at the temple site before she could present herself to the sage and bestow her blessings upon him.

According to local folklore, it is believed that when Lord Shiva wandered the Earth carrying Sati's body, a part of her fell at the location of the temple.

One day, while the priest was cleaning the statue, he noticed bloodstains. Upon confirming with an elder woman in his family, she verified that the Goddess was indeed bleeding. Since that day, the town has observed a ritual of closing the temple for three days and relocating the idol to another section of the temple. On the fourth day, a procession takes place, where the Goddess's idol is carried on an elephant, accompanied by musicians, for a ritual bath in the Mithra River.

Another elephant carrying the idol of Lord Shiva awaits in front of the temple for Goddess Parvati's return after her ritual bath. A magnificent ceremony follows, during which the two idols are reinstalled in the temple, and devotees offer prayers to the Goddess's stained dress.

Today, it is believed that the Goddess used to menstruate monthly, although such occurrences are now infrequent. Nevertheless, the priest continues the tradition of verifying this with the eldest woman in his household.

1. Goddess Parvati and Feminine Energy

- The Chengannur Mahadeva Temple is dedicated to Lord Shiva, but it also features a significant representation of **Goddess Parvati**, who is the consort of Shiva. The temple emphasizes the duality and balance of divine masculine and feminine energies. Parvati, as a representation of Shakti (the divine feminine), symbolizes fertility, motherhood, and the natural cycles of life, including menstruation.

2. Rituals and Menstruation

- In the temple's practices, menstruation is acknowledged as a natural and sacred process. The temple rituals reflect an understanding of the sacredness of womanhood. While specific practices may vary, the acknowledgment of women's cycles within temple rituals can create a more inclusive spiritual environment, respecting and honouring the feminine experience.

3. Sacredness of Menstruation

- The temple is believed to have a connection to various Shakti Peethas, places where parts of the goddess Sati are said to have fallen. This association links the temple to the broader context of female divine energy and its recognition within Hinduism. Menstruation, often viewed through a lens of taboo in many cultures, is regarded here as a sacred and vital aspect of life that aligns with the worship of feminine deities.

4. Community Practices

- In many Hindu communities, menstruating women traditionally observe certain restrictions or participate in specific rituals. However, temples like Chengannur Mahadeva Temple can help reshape perceptions around menstruation, offering a space where women feel accepted and valued during their menstrual cycles.

5. Menstruation in Local Beliefs

- There are local customs and beliefs regarding menstruation that may find expression within the temple's community. These can include rituals that honour feminine energy, celebrate women's contributions, and promote understanding and acceptance of menstruation as a natural part of life.

6. Cultural Significance

- The temple serves as a community center where traditional practices are maintained, and discussions around menstruation and womanhood can help break down societal taboos. By honouring feminine deities and recognizing the menstrual cycle, the temple promotes a more positive narrative around women's health and spirituality.

Chengannur Mahadeva Temple embodies a rich tapestry of devotion that honours both Lord Shiva and Goddess Parvati, acknowledging the sacredness of femininity and menstruation. Through its rituals and community practices, the temple contributes to a deeper understanding and acceptance of women's experiences, fostering a spiritual space where feminine energy is celebrated and revered.

CHAPTER TEN

FOLKLORES and MENSTRUATION

Bhagvad Gita Ch18
Verse 31:

ययाधर्ममधर्मंचकार्यंचाकार्यमवेच |
अयथावत्प्रजानातिबुद्धिः सापार्थराजसी||

"The intellect is considered in the mode of passion when it is confused between righteousness and unrighteousness, and cannot distinguish between right and wrong conduct"

Folklore surrounding goddesses and the concept of first menstruation is rich and diverse across various cultures. Many stories celebrate the transition from girlhood to womanhood, highlighting the sacredness of this life milestone. Here's an exploration of folklore related to goddesses and the themes of first menstruation:

1. The Goddess and the Moon

The connection between goddesses and the moon has deep roots in various cultures, symbolizing femininity, fertility, and the cyclical nature of life. Below is a story that illustrates this relationship in the context of menstruation, highlighting the sacredness of this natural process and its ties to divine feminine energy.

The Goddess of the Moon and the Coming of Womanhood

In an ancient land, where the mountains kissed the sky and rivers flowed like silver veins through the earth, there lived a radiant goddess named **Luna**. Luna was the goddess of the moon, often depicted as a beautiful woman with a shimmering gown that reflected the light of the night sky. She watched over the women of the world, guiding them through the cycles of life and nature.

As Luna waxed and waned in the sky, so too did the lives of the women on earth reflect her cycles. The full moon symbolized fertility, love, and abundance, while the new moon represented rest, reflection, and the promise of new beginnings. Each month, when Luna reached her full glory, she bestowed blessings upon the women, empowering them to embrace their femininity and the sacredness of their bodies.

One day, a young girl named **Asha** approached the sacred grove where Luna was said to descend to the earth. Asha was on the cusp of womanhood, feeling the stirrings of change within her. As she stepped into the moonlit grove, she felt a sense of peace envelop her, and she knew that Luna was nearby.

As Asha knelt beneath the glowing moon, she whispered her fears and dreams into the night. She spoke of her upcoming transition, the first menstruation that would mark her passage into womanhood. Suddenly, the air shimmered, and Luna appeared before her, radiant and benevolent.

"Asha," Luna said, her voice as soft as the breeze, "you are on the brink of a great transformation. Your first menstruation is not just a physical change; it is a sacred rite that connects you to the cycles of the earth and the universe. Just as I wax and wane, so too will you experience the cycles of life."

With that, Luna shared the story of her own journey. She told Asha how she, too, had once been a young girl, learning to embrace her femininity and the power of creation within her. "Menstruation is a natural part of your existence, a reminder of the strength you possess as a woman. It is a time to honour your body, to celebrate the life-giving energy within you."

Luna instructed Asha to gather her friends and celebrate this new phase of life. "Create a ritual of joy," she said. "Dance under the moonlight, share stories of your ancestors, and honour the goddess within you and among your sisters."

Asha felt a surge of excitement and empowerment. With Luna's guidance, she gathered her friends and family for a celebration beneath the full moon. They adorned themselves with flowers and painted their faces with symbols of the moon and stars. As they danced and sang, they shared stories of their own experiences, fostering a bond of support and love.

As the night unfolded, Asha felt the energy of the moon flowing through her, and she embraced the changes within her. She understood that menstruation was not a taboo or a burden; it was a blessing, a cycle that connected her to the divine and to all women throughout history.

From that day on, Asha and her friends celebrated their journeys into womanhood with the full moon, honouring Luna and the sacredness of their bodies. They understood that just as the moon cycles through its phases, so too would their lives ebb and flow, filled with the beauty and strength of womanhood.

The story of Asha and Luna reminds us of the deep connection between goddesses, the moon, and menstruation. It emphasizes the importance of celebrating this natural process and recognizing the divine feminine energy that exists within every woman. By embracing these cycles, women can cultivate strength, wisdom, and a sense of community as they navigate their journeys through life.

2. The Story of Demeter and Persephone

The story of **Demeter** and **Persephone** is a rich and powerful myth from ancient Greek mythology that explores themes of motherhood, the cycle of life, death, and rebirth, and the deep connection between women and the earth. This myth beautifully illustrates the journey from girlhood to womanhood, including the significance of menstruation.

The Myth of Demeter and Persephone

Characters

- **Demeter**: The goddess of the harvest, fertility, and agriculture. She represents motherhood, nurturing, and the earth's bounty.

- **Persephone**: The daughter of Demeter, a beautiful maiden associated with spring, flowers, and new life.

One day, while Persephone was playing in a meadow, gathering flowers, she came across a stunning blossom that captivated her. As she reached for it, the earth suddenly opened up, and **Hades**, the god of the underworld, emerged in his chariot. He had fallen in love with Persephone and abducted her to be his queen in the underworld.

When Demeter discovered that her beloved daughter was missing, she was overcome with grief. She searched the earth tirelessly, calling out for Persephone, but she could not find her. In her sorrow, Demeter neglected her duties as the goddess of harvest, and the earth began to wither. Crops failed, and famine spread across the land.

Desperate to find Persephone, Demeter descended into the depths of the earth, visiting every corner of the realm. She eventually learned from **Hecate**, the goddess of magic and witchcraft, that Hades had taken Persephone to the underworld. In her fury, Demeter approached Zeus, the king of the gods, demanding that he return her daughter to her.

Zeus, recognizing the dire situation on earth, agreed to intervene. He sent Hermes, the messenger god, to the underworld to bring Persephone back to Demeter. However, before she left, Hades offered her a pomegranate. Persephone, unaware

of the consequences, ate six seeds, binding her to the underworld.

The Reunion and the Seasons

When Persephone returned to her mother, Demeter was filled with joy, and life blossomed back into the world. However, because Persephone had eaten the pomegranate seeds, she was required to spend part of the year in the underworld with Hades and part of the year with her mother on earth.

This arrangement led to the creation of the seasons:

- **Spring and Summer**: When Persephone is with Demeter, the earth flourishes, and life thrives. Flowers bloom, crops grow, and warmth spreads across the land.
- **Autumn and Winter**: When Persephone returns to Hades, Demeter mourns, leading to the cold and barren months where the earth is devoid of life.

Symbolism of Menstruation

The story of Demeter and Persephone can be interpreted as a powerful metaphor for the transition from girlhood to womanhood, particularly with regard to menstruation. Persephone's journey to the underworld and her return symbolizes the cyclical nature of life, echoing the monthly cycles experienced by women.

- **Menstruation as a Rite of Passage**: Just as Persephone undergoes a transformation from a girl to the queen of the underworld, young girls experience their own transition with the onset of menstruation, marking the beginning of their reproductive years and their journey into womanhood.
- **Connection to the Earth**: The myth underscores the profound connection between women's bodies and the natural cycles of the earth. Just as Demeter's grief leads to the barren winter, menstruation can symbolize both the pain and beauty of womanhood, encompassing the cycles of creation and destruction.

The story of Demeter and Persephone is a timeless narrative that highlights the bond between mother and daughter, the significance of loss and reunion, and the natural cycles of life. It celebrates femininity and the transformative power of womanhood, serving as a reminder of the sacredness of menstruation and the strength that lies within women as they navigate the various phases of life.

3. Hindu Folklore of Menarche

Hindu folklore surrounding menarche (the first menstruation) is rich with rituals, symbolism, and cultural significance. These stories and practices emphasize the importance of this transition in a girl's life, marking her entry into womanhood and acknowledging the sacredness of femininity.

One popular story involves **Goddess Durga**, who embodies strength, courage, and protection. When a girl first menstruates, she is seen as having received Durga's blessings, marking her readiness to embrace womanhood. Families often perform rituals to honour the goddess, seeking her guidance and protection for the girl as she enters this new phase of life.

Ritusuddhi Ceremony

The Ritusuddhi ceremony, also known as **Menses' Rituals**, is a traditional practice observed in various Hindu communities to celebrate a girl's first menstruation. This ceremony serves as a rite of passage and is often conducted with great reverence and joy.

Folklore: It is believed that during this ceremony, the girl is blessed by divine feminine energies. Families often invite relatives and friends to participate in the celebration, which includes rituals, prayers, and sometimes a feast. The girl may be adorned with new clothes and jewellery, symbolizing her new status.

Goddess Durga

Goddess **Durga** is a prominent figure in Hindu mythology, representing feminine strength, power, and protection. She is often invoked during menarche celebrations.

- **Folklore**: Many believe that when a girl experiences her first menstruation, she embodies the qualities of Durga. It is customary to offer prayers and perform rituals to honour the goddess, seeking her blessings for strength and wisdom as the girl navigates this new phase of life. The ceremony may involve storytelling about Durga's victories over evil forces, reinforcing the idea of empowerment.

The Story of Sita

The story of **Sita**, the beloved heroine of the **Ramayana**, intricately weaves themes of virtue, strength, and the challenges faced by women. While Sita's tale does not explicitly focus on menstruation, it embodies many cultural and symbolic elements related to womanhood and the societal expectations surrounding it. Here's a closer look at Sita's story in relation to menstruation and femininity:

The Tale of Sita

Sita is the daughter of King Janaka of Mithila and is considered the incarnation of the goddess **Lakshmi**. Her birth and early life were celebrated, and she is often depicted as the ideal woman—beautiful, devoted, and virtuous. Sita's marriage to **Rama**, the prince of Ayodhya, is one of the most revered love stories in Hindu mythology.

The pivotal moment in Sita's life comes when she is abducted by **Ravana**, the demon king of Lanka. This act of kidnapping serves as a critical turning point in the narrative. Sita's abduction represents not just a personal tragedy but also the violation of a woman's dignity and autonomy. Sita's kidnapping can symbolize the challenges and societal pressures faced by women, including the loss of agency and the societal taboos surrounding their bodies. The subsequent journey that Sita undergoes highlights her resilience in the face of adversity.

The Agni Pariksha (Trial by Fire)

One of the most significant events in Sita's story is the **Agni Pariksha**, where she is put to the test by Rama upon his victory over Ravana. Rama questions Sita's chastity and purity after her time in captivity. In response, Sita willingly enters a fire, demonstrating her purity and devotion.

Connection to Menstruation: The Agni Pariksha has been interpreted in various ways. Some view it as a commentary on societal expectations regarding women's purity and honour, which can be paralleled to the stigma surrounding menstruation. Just as Sita's worth is questioned due to societal norms, women often face scrutiny and misunderstanding regarding their natural bodily processes.

The Symbol of Strength and Sacrifice

Sita's character embodies strength, resilience, and the sacrifices women make for their families and loved ones. Despite the trials she faces, Sita remains steadfast in her devotion to Rama and upholds her dignity.

Menstruation as Strength: Menstruation, like Sita's trials, is a natural and powerful process. It is often associated with the cycles of life, fertility, and the strength of womanhood. Sita's journey can serve as a metaphor for the menstrual cycle, emphasizing the strength and resilience inherent in every woman. Despite passing the Agni Pariksha, Sita faces rejection from Rama later in the story due to societal pressures and gossip regarding her time spent in Ravana's palace. Ultimately, Sita is forced to leave Rama and seeks refuge in the forest.

This part of Sita's story reflects the societal taboos surrounding women's bodies and choices. It can be seen as a critique of how women's worth is often tied to their perceived purity and adherence to societal norms, much like the stigmas surrounding menstruation and womanhood.

The story of Sita, while not explicitly focused on menstruation, resonates deeply with themes of femininity, societal expectations, and the strength of women. Her journey encapsulates the challenges women face regarding their identities, bodies, and roles in society. Through Sita's trials and triumphs, we can draw parallels to the experiences of women, particularly regarding the natural processes of life, such as menstruation.

By honouring Sita's legacy, we celebrate the strength and resilience of women, encouraging a deeper understanding and respect for the feminine experience, including the sacredness of menstruation.

Breaking Taboos

Hindu folklore around menarche also serves to break societal taboos surrounding menstruation. Many communities are now embracing open discussions about menstrual health and hygiene, challenging the stigma attached to this natural process.

Stories are being retold to highlight the sanctity of menstruation and the need for respect and understanding. Celebrating menarche publicly helps normalize menstruation, fostering a positive attitude toward women's health.

Connection to Nature

In Hindu philosophy, there is a deep connection between women and the earth. Menstruation is often seen as a reflection of natural cycles. Girls are taught to honour their bodies and the earth, understanding that just as the earth goes through cycles of creation and destruction, so too do women experience the cycles of life. This connection reinforces the idea that menstruation is a natural and vital aspect of womanhood.

Hindu folklore surrounding menarche is a beautiful tapestry of rituals, stories, and beliefs that celebrate the transition from girlhood to womanhood. Through the lens of divine feminine energy, empowerment, and community support, these traditions acknowledge the sacredness of menstruation and foster positive attitudes toward women's health. By embracing these rituals and stories, communities continue to honour the strength and resilience of women, nurturing future generations with respect and understanding.

4. Inca Goddess Pachamama

Pachamama, the Inca goddess of the earth, fertility, and agriculture, holds a vital place in Andean culture and mythology. Revered as a nurturing mother figure, Pachamama embodies the connection between nature and humanity, and her worship reflects the importance of fertility—both in the earth and in women. The relationship between Pachamama and menstruation is deeply symbolic and significant within the context of fertility and the cycles of life.

Pachamama: The Earth Mother

Pachamama is often depicted as a nurturing figure who provides for her children, sustaining life through the bounty of the earth. She is associated with agriculture, harvests, and the fertility of the land. In Inca mythology, she is considered the provider of food, water, and the natural resources necessary for life. Her reverence reflects the close connection between the earth and the communities that depend on it.

Menstruation and Pachamama

Menstruation is a natural biological process that signifies fertility and the capacity for new life. In this context, Pachamama embodies the earth's fertility and the life-giving aspects of femininity. Women's menstrual cycles are seen as parallel to the cycles of nature—both are a part of the natural order and contribute to the cycle of life.In traditional Andean practices, women often perform rituals and make offerings to Pachamama during menstruation. Some women believe that the power of Pachamama is particularly strong during this time. They may offer their menstrual blood to the earth as a way of honouring Pachamama and acknowledging their connection to her. This act is seen as a sacred offering that symbolizes the life-giving potential of women.

Just as Pachamama is a reflection of the earth's cycles, menstruation is viewed as a reflection of the cycles of life. In many Andean cultures, menstruating women are believed to possess heightened spiritual energy, and their connection to Pachamama allows them to better understand the rhythms of nature. Women may use this time to meditate, reflect, and connect with the earth.

Healing and Transformation:

Menstruation is also seen as a time of renewal and healing. The shedding of the uterine lining can be viewed as a transformative process, akin to the cycles of the earth where old crops are replaced by new growth. Women who honour Pachamama during menstruation may find solace and strength, drawing upon the goddess's nurturing energy to support them through their experiences. The goddess Pachamama represents the deep connection between femininity, fertility, and the earth in Inca culture. Menstruation, as a natural and sacred process, is honoured within this context, emphasizing the life-giving power of women and their integral role in the cycles of nature. By celebrating menstruation as a manifestation of Pachamama's energy, communities reaffirm the importance of honouring both the feminine experience and the earth, fostering a deeper understanding of the interconnectedness of all life.

5. Native American Folklore

Native American folklore is rich with stories and teachings that center around menstruation, emphasizing its significance in the lives of women and their connection to nature, spirituality, and community. Each tribe has its unique beliefs and practices, but common themes of respect, reverence, and the celebration of femininity often emerge.

Many Native American cultures view menstruation as a sacred and powerful gift. It is seen as a natural cycle that connects women to the earth and the cosmos, and is often regarded with respect rather than shame. In various tribes, menstruation is associated with the life-giving forces of nature. Women are considered to have a special connection to the earth, and their menstrual cycles are viewed as aligned with the natural rhythms of life.

The first menstruation, or menarche, is often celebrated as a significant rite of passage. This transition from girlhood to womanhood is marked by ceremonies that include teachings about womanhood, spirituality, and cultural responsibilities. Some tribes hold ceremonies that bring together women and girls to honour this transition. These gatherings often involve storytelling, dancing, and the sharing of wisdom from elders, creating a supportive community atmosphere.

Many Native American tribes draw connections between menstruation, the lunar cycles, and the earth's natural rhythms. Women's menstrual cycles are often believed to be synchronized with the phases of the moon, symbolizing renewal and life. Stories may illustrate how women's cycles mirror the moon's phases, reinforcing the idea that menstruation is a natural and essential part of life's cycles. Some tribes may even encourage women to align their menstrual cycles with the new moon, which symbolizes new beginnings.

During menstruation, women are often regarded as possessing heightened spiritual energy. This time can be seen as an opportunity for introspection and connection to the divine. Women may engage in rituals or solitude during menstruation to connect with their inner selves and the natural world. This sacred time is often viewed as a moment for reflection and renewal. Menstrual blood is often seen as powerful and sacred, symbolizing fertility and the ability to create life. This perspective emphasizes the strength and nurturing aspects of femininity. In some stories, menstrual blood is regarded as a potent life force, and women may use it in rituals or offerings to honor the earth and the spirits. It is celebrated as a vital aspect of womanhood and a connection to the cycles of life.

Education about menstruation is an essential aspect of many Native American cultures. Elders often play a crucial role in teaching young girls about their bodies, the significance of their menstrual cycles, and the responsibilities that come with womanhood. Folktales may be used to impart lessons on respect for oneself, the natural world, and the importance of honouring one's body. These stories help foster a positive understanding of menstruation and womanhood.

Native American folklore surrounding menstruation reflects a deep reverence for the natural processes of life and the sacredness of femininity. Through rituals, stories, and teachings, these cultures honour the transition into womanhood, celebrate the cycles of nature, and recognize the unique strength and healing abilities of women. By embracing these traditions, Native American communities continue to uphold the importance of menstruation as a vital aspect of life, spirituality, and identity.

6. African Folklore

Ma'at, the ancient Egyptian goddess of truth, balance, and cosmic order, plays a vital role in the spiritual and cultural landscape of ancient Egypt. While Ma'at is not directly associated with menstruation in the same way as some other deities, her principles and attributes can be intertwined with themes related to femininity, fertility, and the cycles of life, including menstruation. Here's an exploration of Ma'at's connection to menstruation and what she represents:

Ma'at embodies the concepts of truth, balance, and harmony in the universe. She is often depicted as a woman with an ostrich feather on her head, symbolizing truth and justice. The concept of balance is significant in many aspects of life, including the natural cycles experienced by women. Menstruation is a cyclical process that reflects the natural order of life. Just as Ma'at represents balance in the universe, the menstrual cycle can symbolize the balance within a woman's body, connecting her to the earth and the rhythms of nature.

Ma'at is sometimes associated with fertility, as her principles of order and balance can extend to the cycles of reproduction and motherhood. In ancient Egypt, fertility was often linked to the goddess's teachings about living in harmony with the natural world. Although not specifically tied to menstruation, Ma'at's association with fertility underscores the importance of understanding and respecting the feminine cycle as a natural part of life. This recognition aligns with many ancient cultures that revered women's bodies as vital to the cycle of life and creation.

In ancient Egyptian belief systems, cleanliness and purity were essential concepts tied to the worship of the gods. Women often engaged in rituals of purification, especially during their menstrual cycles, which were viewed as periods requiring spiritual attention and care. Women might have performed purification rituals in honour of Ma'at to maintain spiritual balance and harmony during menstruation. Such practices would reflect a desire to honor the goddess and seek her guidance during this natural process.

Ma'at's teachings emphasized the importance of women in maintaining social order and balance within the community. Women were seen as integral to the family unit, and their roles as nurturers and caretakers were highly respected. In some traditions, menstruation was celebrated as a rite of passage into womanhood, recognizing the significance of this natural process in a woman's life. By honouring Ma'at, women could affirm their roles and responsibilities in maintaining balance within their families and society.

Ma'at's principles extend beyond earthly life to encompass the cosmic order, which included the cycles of the moon and the natural rhythms of the universe. The moon's phases have often been linked to women's menstrual cycles, reflecting the interconnectedness of life.

Just as Ma'at embodies cosmic balance, the menstrual cycle can be viewed as a reflection of the moon's cycles, illustrating the deep connection between women, nature, and the cosmos.

While the goddess Ma'at may not have a direct association with menstruation, her principles of balance, truth, and cosmic order resonate with the natural cycles of femininity and the menstrual experience. By embodying these themes, Ma'at offers a framework for understanding and respecting the sacredness of the menstrual cycle, highlighting its role in the broader context of life, fertility, and spiritual balance. Through her teachings, women can find empowerment, recognizing their bodies as integral to the cycles of nature and the balance of the universe.

CHAPTER ELEVEN

MENSTRUATION AS TAPAS

Bhagvad Gita Ch 18
Verse 33:

धतृ्यायययाधारयतमेन:प्राणने्द्रयिक्रयिा: |
योगनेाव्यभचिारण्ियाधतृि: सापार्थसात्त्वकिी ||

"The steadfast willpower that is developed through Yog, and which sustains the activities of the mind, the life-airs, and the senses, is said to be determination in the mode of goodness."

An often-overlooked aspect of menstruation in Hindu scriptures is its interpretation as a period of austerity (Tapas) and self-purification. Without understanding this context, discussions about menstruation in Hinduism can become incomplete or even misleading.

In Hinduism, **Tapas**—austerity or discipline—is central to achieving both material success and spiritual liberation. It refers to the voluntary hardships one undergoes to reach a goal. This can involve restraining the body, mind, and senses, helping individuals cultivate detachment from worldly pleasures and mental impurities like anger and desire.

Scriptures emphasize that through Tapas, impurities of both body and mind are destroyed, leading to self-purification. This principle of austerity is ingrained in various Hindu rituals, such as rites of passage (Samskaras) and daily practices like meditation and fasting, all designed to aid in self-discipline and detachment.

Menstruation, according to Hindu texts, aligns with this concept of Tapas. Certain restrictions during menstruation—such as refraining from adorning the body, avoiding sexual relations, and abstaining from certain foods—are seen as ways to help women develop self-restraint and detach from material pleasures.

Beyond these prescribed practices, menstruation itself is viewed as a self-purifying process. It cleanses not just the physical body but also the vital energy and mind, freeing women from mental and emotional impurities. This purifying aspect of menstruation is highlighted in stories like that of Indra's sin, where women are described as taking on a portion of the sin and cleansing it through their menstrual cycle.

This belief of menstruation as a self-purifying course that frees one from papa (sin) incurred from Adharmic activities can be drawn back to the Vedas.

It is evident that menstrual discharge consists not only of blood but also the unfertilized egg. In essence, the monthly cycle represents a failure of conception, a missed opportunity for childbirth. In Hindu tradition, bearing children is not merely a duty for householders but is also considered a deeply Dharmic act. By giving birth, a couple empowers a soul (Jivaatma) to enter the physical world and endure its Karmic journey. On the contrary, preventing the birth of a Jivaatma, whether intentionally or unintentionally, is regarded as Adharma, since it deprives the soul of its chance to experience life in the physical realm—an act likened to the severity of taking a life

If one were to inquire how a person prevents a Jivaatma from being born, the answer would involve two scenarios:

a) abortion and

b) the non-fertilization of the egg.

The former is referred to as 'Brunahatya,' which means the killing of an embryo, and is regarded as murder. Hindu scriptures classify this act as one of the gravest sins, associating it with Brahmahatya. Similarly, the non-fertilization of the egg every month leads to a missed prospect for birth and is also linked to

Adharma. The key discrepancy between abortion and the non-fertilization of the egg lies in the severity of the Adharma involved. The severity is greater in the case of abortion, as it involves the termination of an embryo that is on the path to becoming a child.

In contrast, non-fertilization simply results in the left-over of an egg that was projected to unite with sperm. This consideration is crucial for rendering the story of Indra and how women bear one-third of the sin associated with Brahmahatya, which rises from the egg's failure to impregnate and thus not becoming a suitable host for a Jivaatma to enter the physical realm.

The story does not end with women taking upon themselves one-third paapa from Indra. It further says that as a result of women inheriting this one-third paapa of Brahmahatya, they had to menstruate once every month and after menstruation they would become fertile again. In other words, menstruation acted as a purification process, which helped women get rid of the paapa they had inherited. Thus, there is a clear indication in the Vedas itself about menstruation being a self-purifying process and among other things, it frees women from the paapam incurred due to non-fertilization of their egg.

This concept is further detailed in the Smritis and the Dharmasutras.

Angirasa Smriti (Verse 42)

"वैश्यनेतुग्रदास्पृष्टःशुनाशूद्रणेवाद्वजिः.
उपोष्यरजनीमकेांपंज्चगव्यनेशुध्यतिं".

explicitly means that women become purified due to menstruation.

Manu Smriti (5.108)

अद्भरि्गात्राणिशुध्यन्तमिनःसत्यनेशुध्यतिा
वद्यातपोभ्याम्भूतात्माबुद्धरि्ज्ञाननेशुध्यतिा॥
मनुस्मृतिः

Which translates to women whose thoughts have become impure, will be purified by menstruation.

Therefore, when it is stated that menstruation purifies women, it signifies the liberation of women from a wide array of Adharmic actions committed through their body, mind, and speech. It also encompasses the release from feelings of guilt and shame linked to distressing experiences such as rape and sexual assault. However, this does not imply that women are exempt from karmic repercussions or that they can engage in any Adharma without consequences.

Menstruation does not serve as a free pass that absolves women from any Adharmic activities, irrespective of their severity. Rather, its self-purifying influence is limited to a broad range of Adharmas committed through body, mind, and speech on a everyday basis, primarily inadvertently or in unavoidable circumstances. It does not spread to intentional Adharmas of important magnitude carried out for selfish motives without regard for the consequences. Nonetheless, despite this limitation, menstruation remains a highly beneficial means of self-purification and is a privilege that is uniquely available to women.

Men do not experience menstruation and, therefore, lack access to this self-purifying process. In contrast, scriptures outline various rules and ritual practices tailored to one's Varna (inherent qualities) and Ashrama (stage of life). Activities such as Samskaras, Mantra Japa, and Sandhopasana are prescribed for men to achieve purity and liberation from Adharmic actions. Women, however, do not need to engage in these spiritual practices to attain purity; they naturally achieve it through menstruation. What requires special effort for men comes to women as part of their biological process. This unique aspect of menstruation and the privilege it confers upon women is emphasized repeatedly in Hindu scriptures.

Baudhayana Dharmasutra (2.2.4.4), for instance, says: "Women (possess) an unrivalled means of purification; they never become (entirely) impure. For month by month their temporary uncleanness removes their sins."

The same is repeated in **Vashishta Dharmasutra** (28.4), which further explains this and says Women are under the protection of Soma, Gandharva, and Agni, who each bestow cleanliness, a melodious voice, and purity of body, respectively, ensuring that women remain free from impurities. Soma, one of the names for the Moon, is closely linked to the menstrual cycle. Agni, associated with the mind, acts as a witness and purifier of all our actions. Gandharva is directly connected to speech. Together, Soma, Agni, and Gandharva are the divine guardians of physical, verbal, and mental actions. Through these deities, menstruation brings purity to a woman's body, mind, and speech. The verses emphasize that, through the influence of these three deities related to different aspects of purification, women are "free from stains and not contaminated."

Hindu scriptures clearly convey that menstruation is a privilege that helps women maintain purity in their body, mind, and speech. However, like any form of Tapas or austerity, menstruation comes with specific rules and restrictions that individuals should strive to follow. Without adhering to these guidelines, one may not fully reap the benefits of the practice.

In other words, while menstruation has the potential to bring purity and relieve women of demerits, this benefit can be compromised if they do not fully understand its austere and purifying nature and fail to follow the practices outlined in the scriptures. Without this awareness and adherence, women may only experience partial benefits from the menstruation process and may not achieve complete freedom from impurities at all levels.

Thus, menstruation is seen as both an act of austerity and a natural means of purification, enabling women to cleanse themselves of various forms of sin (Adharma) and uphold purity in body, mind, and spirit. This distinctive aspect of menstruation in a woman's life is regarded as a privilege, granting her a level of purification that men must achieve through intentional spiritual efforts involving rituals and practices. The Hindu scriptures portray menstruation not as a period of impurity, but as a significant time for purification and spiritual renewal, especially when approached with the right understanding and respect.

What we consider impure is just as sacred as what we view as pure.

Impurity as Auspiciousness

Here are a few examples from the Sridurgasaptashati (Devi Mahatmyam), Tantroktam Ratrisuktam, Lalita Sahasranama, and Vedoktam Ratri Suktam (Rigveda X.127.1-8).

Pañcapretamañcādhiśāyinī, meaning "She rests on a couch made of five corpses," illustrates a profound concept. In daily life, we associate ritual impurity with death, such as when a family member passes away or during funerals. Those who have lost a parent are often prohibited from entering a temple for a certain period due to this ritual impurity. Additionally, there are various purification rituals observed after being near or handling a dead body, or attending a funeral. Yet, the Goddess herself rests in this "impure" place—on that very symbol of mortality that often evokes fear. This reminds us of goddesses like Kali and Tara, who dwell in the cremation grounds. Even in the most "impure" places, the embodiment of divine auspiciousness is present.

Yā devī sarvabhūteṣu tṛṣnārūpeṇa saṁsthitā, meaning "To the goddess who abides in all beings in the form of attachment," highlights the Goddess not just as the force of creative desire, but also as the one who binds us to the material world and keeps us attached to the cycle of life and death. This attachment makes us forget our true divinity and inner worth. Similarly, Durgamohā, "She who causes deep delusion," represents her presence even in the confusion that leads us astray. The Goddess, symbolizing auspiciousness, resides even in what we consider "impure" thoughts or emotions.

There are specific examples related to menstruation found in various texts. In the writings of the yogini Lakshminkara, she instructs practitioners to draw Devi mandalas using vermillion, which she refers to as "the menstrual blood of the earth." Consider the reaction of many Hindus today upon reading this quote from the Chandamaharoshana-tantra: "A man should regard every substance discharged from a woman's body as pure and should be willing to touch it and ingest it if requested." Whether this statement is intended to be taken literally or as a challenge to those of us navigating a patriarchal society is open to interpretation. Nevertheless, it's evident that menstrual fluids, along with other bodily excretions, are associated with a sense of sacredness.

If one wants to know how can we recognize auspiciousness even within what is traditionally considered impure? David Frawley, also known as Pandit Vamadeva Shastri, offers an insightful example in his book Inner Tantric Yoga to illustrate this point:

Prana embodies the Goddess within us. Worshipping prana as Shakti may be the highest form of devotion, transforming life into a sacred ritual where thought itself becomes prayer and mantra. Our urinary and excretory organs serve as the means by which the body expresses the purifying aspects of water and earth.

In this meditation, concentrate on the power that enables you to release water from the body through urination, and similarly with the process of excretion. Reflect on the source of the impulse behind these vital urges. It originates from a pranic urge, akin to an electrical impulse. Consider where this impulse enters the mind and where the energy resides in potential when these vital functions are inactive. Learn to connect with that pranic force. Recognize the creative energy present in all reproductive processes, including menstruation. Embrace this creative energy while letting go of the forms it produces. Allow that energy to renew both your body and mind. Remember, this energy belongs to prana, not just to the motor organs, which are merely instruments of expression.

In her study of Hindu communities in Orissa, India, Frederique Apffel-Marglin uncovered some fascinating perspectives from the men of the region regarding menstruation. A villager explained the significance of the Raja Parba festival, which marks the symbolic menstruation of the goddess Harachandi: "The Mother, the earth, is bleeding... We believe that women are also symbolically bleeding at this time, as the Mother bleeds through them. During the earth's menses, women don't work; they sing and play with their friends. The purpose is for them to rest, just as they do during their monthly periods. They should not be disturbed or touched. When the Goddess is bleeding, we too stop working in the fields—not just farmers, but all men. It is our duty to honor the Goddess and women at this time. Young women celebrate Raja because they are the center of creation, and we want to make them happy."

The women in the village share an equally interesting view. They describe menstruation not as something that passively happens to them, but as an action they perform, a process that aligns them with cosmic rhythms. For them, menstruation is an active, empowering experience rather than something their bodies impose on them.

The issue isn't in viewing menstruation as a time of ritual impurity, but in seeing women as objects to be controlled or as less than divine. This perspective leads to the misconception that women incite inauspiciousness. Casteism, patriarchy, and an unease with our inner feminine contribute to greater repression and avoidance of things seen as impure or unpredictable.

Menstruation highlights the powerful aspects of the divine feminine—its mystery, pain, and intuition, which stand in contrast to logic. By avoiding menstruation, we are avoiding what confuses or challenges us. Yet, these qualities, when embraced, can foster spiritual and psychological growth. Breaking free from the superstitions that aim to control these elements allows us to connect more deeply with ourselves.

Deciding which customs to keep and which to discard requires introspection. Menstrual practices vary widely, even within families, creating an opportunity for meaningful dialogue among women. Generally, the most consistent guidelines involve participation in rituals like puja and homa, or preparing prasadam, but customs about entering temples or attending religious events differ. For instance, not participating in your own wedding because of menstruation likely doesn't hold up. Historically, the rules are more about strong recommendations than about incurring "bad karma."

As for men, menstruation customs are not for them to impose. Menstruating individuals hold more authority over what feels intuitively right for them. There's no universal rule to follow during this time—some may need space, while others may seek comfort.

While some experience pain, others don't. Avoiding your partner during this time or blaming every irritation on PMS is not helpful. Instead, empathy and communication foster healthier relationships.

In my opinion, social customs around the menstrual cycle often stemmed from men's fear of what they didn't understand about women. This fear led to taboos aimed at controlling women's nature. However, women themselves likely contributed to these customs, using them as a way to gain space, rest, and rejuvenation, and to assert their own values. In some cases, these practices were initiated by women for protection and to honor their need for balance and rest.

Customs surrounding menstruation can also serve as an opportunity for women to tap into their natural instinct and intuition, which are closely linked to their embodiment of the Divine Feminine. Many women have experienced moments where they've mentally "asked" their body to delay their period for a more convenient time—like postponing it from Saturday to Sunday—and found that it actually worked. This recurring phenomenon suggests that menstruation connects us to a deep body-wisdom beyond just the emotional and physical detox it brings.

You don't need to go as far as collecting menstrual blood in a jar and worshipping it, but it's important to avoid fostering negative attitudes toward menstruation, such as viewing the associated pain as unnecessary, disgusting, or meaningless. There is a balance to be struck where we can regard our bodies and their processes as sacred and natural without obsessing over them in either a negative or overly glorified way.

It's easy to see divinity in the beauty of the world, to admire the "roses" in life. But true growth comes when we also recognize the divine in the challenging, painful, and confusing aspects of life, embracing them as opportunities for deep emotional and spiritual development.

CHAPTER TWELVE

CONTEMPORARY EPOCH IN THE MEN'S WORLD

Bhagvad Gita Ch 18
Verse:13
अन्तःप्रविष्टःशास्ताजनानांसर्वात्मा
तस्मैनमःकरुणारूपायवेदात्मनेहरये

"Salutations to the compassionate Lord, who resides in the hearts of all beings and understands their innermost nature."

The above mentioned verse can inspire men to be compassionate and understanding toward the natural processes that women go through, including menstruation. It suggests that empathy and respect should guide interactions and understanding of bodily processes in both men and women.

In many cultures, menstruation has historically been shrouded in stigma, but modern times are changing, and discussions around menstruation are becoming more open. There's increasing emphasis on educating young girls about menstrual hygiene, body positivity, and dispelling myths or taboos related to menstruation.

From a mother's perspective, guiding a daughter through this transition is a deeply emotional experience. It can be an opportunity for bonding, sharing wisdom, and teaching self-care. Mothers might share their own experiences to make their daughters feel more comfortable, providing both practical advice on hygiene and emotional support.

Men can hold a range of perspectives on menstruation, varying from limited awareness to a genuine wish to offer support.

Limited understanding: Some men may lack sufficient knowledge about menstruation and its impact on women. This often stems from the perception that menstruation is solely a women's issue and not something that men need to comprehend.

Unfavourable perceptions: Insufficient knowledge can result in negative attitudes and feelings of discomfort.

Willingness to offer support: Men can support women during their menstrual cycles in various ways, including:

- Being unfazed by menstrual stains or the knowledge that a woman is menstruating.
- Being tender during intimacy when a woman is in her ovulatory phase.
- Buying menstrual products for a partner, sister, or mother
- Providing a soothing abdominal massage or placing a hot water bottle on the abdomen to alleviate menstrual discomfort.

Conversely, men's understanding of menstruation has significantly evolved over time, shaped by cultural, social, and educational influences. Historically, menstruation was often surrounded by mystery and stigma, but contemporary conversations increasingly focus on the importance of awareness, empathy, and open dialogue about this natural biological process. Men's perceptions of menstruation are frequently influenced by cultural beliefs and societal norms. In many cultures, menstruation has been treated as a taboo topic, leading to misconceptions and a lack of knowledge about the biological processes involved. Traditionally, menstruation was linked to myths and negative connotations, creating discomfort or embarrassment for both women and men. This stigma often resulted in limited discussions and education regarding menstruation. Education is crucial in shaping men's understanding of this topic. Recently, there has been a movement toward more comprehensive sex education that includes discussions about menstruation, fostering a better understanding among both genders. Today, many men are more knowledgeable about menstruation thanks to educational initiatives, conversations with partners, and exposure to media that normalize the subject. This increased awareness helps dispel myths and reduces stigma.

As societal perceptions of menstruation evolve, many men are increasingly showing empathy and support for the women in their lives. A better understanding of menstruation can enhance relationships and strengthen partnerships. Educated men can offer both emotional and practical support to their partners during their menstrual cycles, helping to ease discomfort and fostering open communication about needs and feelings. Discussions about menstruation are becoming more prevalent, contributing to the dismantling of taboos around the subject. This cultural transformation encourages men to participate in these conversations and share their view points. Men's knowledge of the biological processes involved in menstruation can vary widely. Some men may have a basic understanding, while others may have more in-depth knowledge based on education or personal experiences. Understanding the physiological aspects of menstruation—such as hormonal changes, symptoms, and the menstrual cycle—can help men appreciate the complexity of women's health and the significance of menstruation in women's lives. Media representations of menstruation can also influence men's understanding. Increased visibility of menstruation in television, films, and social media has contributed to normalizing the subject and educating wider audiences. When menstruation is portrayed realistically and sensitively in popular culture, it can encourage men to engage with the topic, challenge stereotypes, and foster a more informed understanding of women's experiences.

Understanding menstruation among men is a multifaceted issue that encompasses cultural perceptions, education, empathy, and communication. As societal attitudes continue to evolve, more men are gaining awareness of the significance of menstruation and its impact on women's lives. So to simplify; girls and women usually have their periods from three to five days. Besides bleeding from the vagina, they may have:

- Abdominal Pain
- Lower back pain
- Bloating
- Food cravings
- Mood swings
- Headache and fatigue
- Premenstrual syndrome [PMS]

Men's contribution to the understanding and support of menstruation is vital in fostering a more inclusive and supportive environment for women. While men do not experience menstruation directly, their involvement can significantly impact attitudes, perceptions, and the overall experience surrounding this natural biological process.

1. Education and Awareness

Men can play an essential role in educating themselves and others about menstruation. This includes understanding the biological processes involved, recognizing the emotional and physical challenges women may face, and dispelling myths associated with menstruation.

- **Personal Research**: Men can take the initiative to learn about menstruation through books, online resources, or educational programs. This knowledge helps them engage in meaningful conversations and challenge misconceptions.

2. Open Communication

Encouraging open dialogue about menstruation can create a more supportive environment. Men can foster discussions with their partners, friends, and family, helping to normalize the topic and reduce stigma.

- **Active Listening**: By listening to women's experiences and concerns about menstruation, men can demonstrate empathy and understanding. This can help women feel more comfortable discussing their needs and feelings.

3. Emotional Support

Men can provide emotional support to the women in their lives during their menstrual cycles. This support can take various forms, including offering comfort, understanding, and validation of the physical and emotional challenges that may arise.

- **Offering Help**: Men can be proactive in offering assistance during difficult times, whether by providing pain relief, running errands, or simply being there to listen.

4. Promoting Inclusivity

Men can advocate for inclusive conversations about menstruation, challenging the societal taboos that often surround it. This advocacy can lead to greater awareness and understanding within their communities.

- **Challenging Stereotypes**: By speaking out against negative stereotypes and cultural taboos related to menstruation, men can help create a more accepting atmosphere for discussing this natural process.

5. Supporting Menstrual Health Initiatives

Men can contribute to menstrual health initiatives and organizations that promote education, awareness, and access to menstrual products. This involvement can help address issues related to menstrual hygiene and health equity.

- **Volunteering or Donating**: Men can volunteer their time or resources to support organizations that provide menstrual products to those in need or educate communities about menstrual health.

6. Understanding the Impact on Relationships

Men can recognize how menstruation can affect relationships, both romantically and within families. Being aware of these dynamics allows them to navigate situations more thoughtfully and sensitively.

- **Adapting to Changes**: Understanding that menstrual cycles can influence mood, energy levels, and physical well-being can help men adapt their behaviour and communication, fostering a more harmonious relationship.

7. Incorporating Menstrual Awareness in Education

Men can support initiatives that incorporate menstrual education into school curricula, ensuring that future generations have a better understanding of menstruation from a young age.

- **Advocating for Comprehensive Education**: Men can advocate for comprehensive sex education that includes information on menstruation, encouraging schools to address this essential topic.

Men's contributions to the understanding and support of menstruation are crucial in creating a more empathetic and inclusive society. By educating themselves, fostering open communication, providing emotional support, and advocating for menstrual health initiatives, men can help normalize discussions about menstruation and reduce the stigma surrounding it. This collective effort promotes a healthier and more supportive environment for women and contributes to gender equality in conversations about health and well-being.

Pain During Menstruation

Are period cramps really that bad?

This is how we often hear that question: *ArE cRaMpS rEaLlY tHaT BaD?* And the answer is: Yes, they can indeed be that bad.

Describing menstrual cramps to someone who has never experienced them can be challenging—similar to trying to explain the sensation of getting hit in the 'crown jewels' to someone with a different anatomy.

But let's give it a shot: It feels like someone is tightly gripping and squeezing your organs from the inside. The pain can vary significantly, but it's common to feel the uterus contracting, often accompanied by sharp pains or a dull ache. Ever experienced a stomach bug? It feels somewhat similar, but the discomfort is located lower in your abdomen. Intense menstrual cramps and bloating can also indicate an underlying condition. If the pain becomes debilitating or suddenly worsens, it's crucial to consult a healthcare provider.

As if cramps and bleeding weren't challenging enough, periods can also bring along lower back pain, nausea, diarrhoea, and mood fluctuations.

The first thing any father, son or brother should understand is these periodic cycles can come with lot of traumatic bodily adjustments varying as per different people, lifestyles, genetics, etc.

Over half of women experience some level of pain during menstruation. However, about 10% endure severe menstrual pain that can last for 1 to 3 days, making it difficult for them to work or even get out of bed. Menstrual pain can be intense and may manifest as cramps in the abdomen, back, and groin, and occasionally in the legs. Some women also experience additional symptoms such as nausea, vomiting, irritability, constipation, and frequent urination. This painful menstruation is essentially a heightened sensitivity in the uterus, occurring as part of the normal menstrual process.

If menstrual pain is extremely severe, affects overall well-being, cannot be managed with standard painkillers, or leads to a loss of productivity, a gynecological evaluation should be conducted, and appropriate treatment should be sought.

The aim of the gynecological examination is to identify any underlying and significant causes of menstrual pain. Generally, secondary dysmenorrhea is observed in women of childbearing age.

Causes of Pains:

- Endometriosis (the inner layer of the uterus is located on the outer surface of the uterus or in a non-uterine area)
- Stenosis in the cervix
- Uterine tumours
- The uterus is in different positions (especially if it is pointed towards the back)
- Inflammatory diseases of the uterus and adjacent organs
- Psychological reasons

Many women may also suffer from **menstrual migraine** apart from their cramps. Menstrual migraine is similar to other types of migraine headaches; however, some women experience severe migraine attacks specifically during their menstrual periods, with headaches being uncommon at other times.

This condition is referred to as menstrual migraine and typically manifests the day before menstruation, lasting for a few days.

These migraines can negatively impact daily life, especially since women are already dealing with the physical strain of menstruation. Hormonal therapy and preventive treatments are often used to alleviate this pain.

Three Ways to Prevent Menstrual Migraine:

1. Maintain a regular sleep schedule.
2. Manage stress effectively.
3. Follow a healthy diet.

Other factors that may trigger migraines before and during menstruation include alcohol consumption, lack of sleep, and hunger.

Now, many of the men may often be confused thinking is it even appropriate to inquire if someone is on their period? Hmm.... As a general guideline, it's best to avoid asking this question. It is frequently posed when a woman seems angry, upset, or having a rough day. The issue here lies in the underlying assumption that her feelings or decisions are irrational and invalid, which can be quite frustrating. However, if your intention is to genuinely help and offer support, then feel free to ask. Other main question men would want to know would be:

What is PMS and why does it lead to mood swings?

I have explained PMS before also, however, this time around I've tried to describe it from a man's understanding perspective. Hopefully it will prove to be successful. Premenstrual Syndrome (PMS) encompasses a range of symptoms that many experience in the week prior to menstruation. These symptoms can vary widely depending on how an individual responds to hormonal fluctuations in their body.

Some people may not experience any PMS symptoms at all, while others can feel them quite intensely. Common PMS symptoms include tearfulness, irritability, and difficulty concentrating. Physical symptoms may also arise, such as fatigue, headaches, cramping, breast tenderness, and cravings for certain foods (chocolate, anyone?).

If someone in your life shares that they're having a tough time with PMS, it's important to be understanding and supportive. Although it can often be minimized or joked about, PMS is a genuine experience that deserves empathy.

How can I be more supportive?

Avoid feeling awkward about it. There's nothing 'dirty' or unhealthy about menstruation. For too long, the shame and stigma surrounding periods—primarily due to a lack of understanding—have made many feel uncomfortable with their bodies and hesitant to seek help.

Here are some practical ways to offer support:

1. **Don't be alarmed by menstrual products:**
   If you come across a box of tampons in the bathroom or see a pad fall out of someone's bag, don't make a fuss. Treat it like you would with earbuds or toilet paper. Even better, offer to buy pads or tampons when grocery shopping. Trust us, no one will assume you've suddenly started your period when they see you at the checkout with menstrual products. In fact, they might wish there were more guys like you!
2. **Stock your bathroom with menstrual products:**
   Running out of pads or tampons or being caught off guard by your period can be frustrating—even for the most seasoned individuals! Be the guy who's comfortable keeping menstrual products in his bathroom cabinet (or car, or backpack). You'll earn instant brownie points.
3. **Speak up for your friends and family:**
   If you find yourself in a situation where people mock or shame others for having a period, don't hesitate to speak up. Educate them about menstruation. This can help dispel common myths and foster a more supportive environment for those who menstruate.

If you feel like your knowledge of menstruation is lacking, keep educating yourself, stay curious, and continue having conversations about it. The more you learn, the better equipped you'll be to support the people in your life who experience periods—whether as a partner, father, brother, colleague, or friend.

CHAPTER THIRTEEN

SHAME OF MENSTRUATION

Bhagvad Gita Ch 18
Verse 39:

यदग्रचेानुबन्धेचसुखंमोहनमात्मनः |
नद्रिालस्यप्रमादोत्थंतत्तामसमुदाहृतम् ||

"That happiness which covers the nature of the self from beginning to end, and which is derived from sleep, indolence, and negligence, is said to be in the mode of ignorance."

In Indian culture, discrimination against menstruating women is widespread, with periods historically viewed as taboo and associated with impurity. Women often face exclusion from social and spiritual events, barred from entering temples and shrines, and even prohibited from the kitchen. From a young age, girls learn to endure the pain and fear of seeking help when experiencing physical and mental discomfort due to menstruation. However, in recent years, the rise of social media has encouraged women to share their experiences and stories related to menstruation.

Despite this newfound freedom, it is often met with skepticism, and individuals sharing their experiences face threats of bans. According to one study, only 36% of India's 355 million menstruating women use sanitary napkins, while the rest rely on old cloths, ash, leaves, mud, and other unsafe materials to manage their menstrual flow. Menstrual health experts note that the coronavirus crisis has exacerbated the situation in India. The country is currently under strict lockdown measures, severely disrupting the production and supply of menstrual hygiene products. This has led to a sanitary pad crisis in India. Moreover, the issue of period poverty extends beyond Indian borders, impacting women worldwide.

Taboos and myths surrounding menstruation, often rooted in Hindu beliefs, significantly affect various aspects of women's lives. The pervasive stigma surrounding menstruation can have detrimental effects on girls' emotional and physical well-being. This lack of awareness stems from deeply ingrained cultural taboos in India. Nearly 75% of women in India resort to using plastic bags or newspapers as alternatives because social pressures make them hesitant to purchase sanitary products. Menstruation remains a largely taboo subject in India, leaving many young girls feeling ashamed of their bodies.

Bhagavad Gita (2.13):

Sanskrit: देहिनोऽस्मिन्यथादेहेकौमारंयौवनंजरा। तथादेहान्तरप्राप्तिर्धीरस्तत्रनमुह्यति॥

Translation: "Just as the soul experiences childhood, youth, and old age in this body, so too it attains another body; the wise are not deluded by this."

Interpretation:

This verse reminds us that bodily changes are a natural part of life. Menstruation, like other bodily processes, is a phase in a woman's life that signifies change and growth. The teachings encourage wisdom and understanding of the physical body without attachment or judgment. Men could take this as a reminder to approach menstruation with empathy, recognizing it as a natural process without stigma or negativity.

The **Gita's** broader message of compassion and equality applies to how all human experiences, including menstruation, should be viewed with respect and understanding. While it may not have a direct reference, the philosophy promotes respecting all aspects of life and embracing the cyclical nature of the body.

The relationship between fathers and daughters with regard to menstruation can be a delicate yet transformative aspect of their bond. Traditionally, discussions around menstruation were often seen as a topic exclusively between mothers and daughters, leaving many fathers distanced from this aspect of their daughters' lives. However, in modern times, fathers are increasingly encouraged to engage in conversations about menstruation, playing an important role in supporting their daughters emotionally and practically during this significant phase of life.

Daughters may feel hesitant or shy to ask their fathers for practical help related to menstruation, such as buying sanitary products. Fathers can make an effort to ensure their daughters have what they need during their periods, whether it's buying supplies or understanding their needs for comfort and care. A father who's informed about menstrual products and cycles can better support his daughter by ensuring that she always has access to what she needs. Being prepared for moments like her first period or unexpected situations shows that he's attentive and involved.

Traditionally, menstruation has been viewed as a "women's issue," but as fathers become more engaged, they challenge gender norms and redefine masculinity by showing that men can and should be part of conversations about women's health. It's time to **Redefine Masculinity**: By being involved, fathers not only foster a closer bond with their daughters but also teach boys and other men in the family that menstruation is not something to shy away from.

Father's role in his daughter's life during puberty can have a lasting impact on her self-esteem and confidence. When a father shows that he respects and understands menstruation, it helps the daughter develop a positive attitude toward her body and her changing identity as a young woman. **Positive Body Image**: Fathers who express pride in their daughters' growth and transition into womanhood help boost their daughters' confidence. This contributes to healthier self-esteem, making daughters feel supported, accepted, and valued during an often-sensitive time.

Single fathers, in particular, may feel challenged when their daughters reach puberty and begin menstruating. However, with openness, education, and the support of other female role models or resources, single fathers can also effectively guide their daughters through this process. **Seeking Resources**: Single fathers can educate themselves through books, health professionals, or female relatives, ensuring they are prepared to offer both emotional and practical support. This fosters a sense of security and confidence in their daughters.

Fathers can play a key role in their daughters' experiences with menstruation, from breaking societal taboos to offering emotional and practical support. By engaging in conversations about menstruation with empathy and openness, fathers contribute to normalizing this natural process and strengthen the bond with their daughters. Through this involvement, they help their daughters develop a positive self-image, confidence, and a healthy understanding of their bodies, ultimately shaping a more inclusive and supportive family dynamic.

CHAPTER FOURTEEN

EMBRACING THE TRUTH

In reclaiming the narrative of menstruation, we break free from centuries of myths and taboos, celebrating the resilience and power of the female body. Menstruation is more than a biological process; it is a symbol of life's cyclical nature, intertwined with creation and renewal. Across cultures, menstruation has been both revered and stigmatized, tied to fertility rituals and sacred practices, while also burdened with taboos that silenced women. By embracing science and cultural histories, we can replace superstition with understanding, fostering respect for menstruation as a vital, life-affirming force. Open dialogue and education allow us to honour its history and reclaim it as a symbol of strength and womanhood.

Menstruation is an immense and deeply sensitive subject, one that encompasses a myriad of issues—both personal and societal. Addressing all of these complexities may well take a lifetime, given the wide-ranging cultural, medical, and emotional dimensions that impact individuals and communities alike. However, it will be my ongoing endeavour to continue this conversation in future works, perhaps in a new form or series. My goal is to bring to light more of the diverse experiences that women encounter—stories that often remain untold but have the power to reshape understanding and foster empathy. These experiences have been transformative for me, opening doors to wisdom and understanding that I never imagined, and I hope to share them in ways that inspire deeper reflection and meaningful change for others.

DESIRED CHANGES IN THE SOCIETY

My dream is to create a world where menstruation is no longer surrounded by shame or stigma, where education and awareness replace outdated traditions that have long held women back. It breaks my heart that in so many remote parts of our country, women still lack basic knowledge about menstrual hygiene. They are forced to use unhygienic methods like old rags, simply because they have no access to or awareness of sanitary pads, let alone menstrual cups, which could make a world of difference in their lives.

Even more troubling is the mindset that persists—where menstruating women are seen as impure, unworthy of touching religious objects, or even entering their own kitchens. These beliefs are perpetuated not just by men, but by the very women who should stand as their allies—the older generations who have been conditioned to accept these practices as part of our culture.

I want to challenge this deep-rooted thinking. It's not enough for us to make sanitary products available if we don't first address the perception of menstruation itself. Periods are a natural, beautiful part of being a woman, a symbol of life and creation. To label it as inauspicious or impure is not only wrong but harmful. My mission is to ensure that every woman, no matter where she is from, understands her worth and is empowered to embrace her femininity without shame.

It's time we rewrite this narrative—not just for the women of today but for the generations to come.

So if were to summarise my book , here is what my thoughts would be:

Many Hindu women often face confusion between being revered as embodiments of Shakti, the divine feminine principle, and being considered impure or unfit to perform religious rituals during menstruation. They are sometimes treated as inauspicious or "dirty" during this time. According to the Manusmriti, a woman is considered ritually impure until her menstrual flow has ceased, with varying interpretations stating this happens after the third, fifth, seventh, or even ninth day. During this period, women are often discouraged from performing puja, entering temples, cooking, or even interacting with their families.

Some argue that these practices exist to allow women to rest during menstruation, which might make sense during the first day or two when energy levels can be low. However, unless a woman is anemic or has low blood pressure, fatigue typically doesn't persist beyond the initial day, and some women experience no fatigue at all. With modern medication that alleviates pain and regulates menstrual flow, these customs seem increasingly out of place, raising the question of their relevance today.

The root issue appears to be the conflation of the terms "impure" and "inauspicious." Many Hindus seem to have mistakenly equated the two, leading to practices that, in the modern context, feel unfair and outdated.

It is true that women are often discouraged from performing puja or participating in certain religious activities, such as handling offerings, during menstruation. While the Manusmriti does make this suggestion, it is important to note that modern Hindus do not view it as an authoritative text, and it was never intended to provide enduring guidelines beyond its historical context.

Nonetheless, there has likely been a long-standing tradition that discourages women from performing puja or homa during their menstrual cycle.

The primary explanation for menstruation practices is related to the regulation of prana, or energy, within the body. Our body contains five types of prana, which can be understood as energy, breath, or life force. These five pranas are: prana, which governs intake; apana, which handles elimination; samana, which aids in assimilation; vyana, responsible for circulation and distribution; and udana, which is linked to expression, particularly through speech. Any obstruction in the flow of these pranas leads to imbalances or illness (for example, an obstruction in samana may result in metabolic or learning disorders). During puja and homa, there is a release of accumulated prana, often causing it to move upwards in the body towards the higher chakras.

It is believed that during menstruation, apana—the prana responsible for downward movement—becomes naturally dominant, and this serves an important purpose. It facilitates the outward flow of physical impurities, such as uterine tissue, as well as the release of repressed emotions, which can manifest as mood swings during PMS. Since religious practices like puja are designed to move prana upwards in the body, engaging in them during menstruation, when the body requires apana to remain dominant, may not be ideal. However, it's worth noting that in most traditions, mental practices like japa (silent repetition of mantras) and manas puja (mental worship) are generally allowed during menstruation, though this may vary depending on one's spiritual tradition or personal beliefs.

Apana involves not only physical excretion but also the release of emotional energy. PMS and menstruation are seen as twelve opportunities each year for individuals with uteruses to confront and release repressed emotions. It is important for menstruating individuals to be mindful and fully experience these emotions as they come to the surface. The emotions that arise during PMS or menstruation are significant, as they reflect genuine and valid emotional truths that have been hidden beneath the surface. These feelings are not imaginary, and women are not viewed as irrational or unstable for experiencing them. The apana energy, which is predominant during menstruation, supports the healthy release of these emotions.

We often avoid confronting our unsettling, confusing, or seemingly irrational emotions, even if they surface just once a month. While it's true that some individuals suffer significantly during and before menstruation due to conditions like PCOS or endometriosis, recognizing this emotional release as a natural part of our detoxification process can be transformative. Allowing these emotions to resurface and be felt—without harming ourselves or others—can become a powerful form of psychological healing. Many menstruating individuals feel the need to retreat from external life and become more introspective during this time. If approached with awareness, this withdrawal offers an opportunity to reconnect with the deeper aspects of one's nature.

This isn't just about taking a break from physically demanding tasks; it's a genuine turning inward, which can feel exhausting before leading to the reward of greater self-awareness and connection to one's inner self. Confronting difficult emotions is a crucial part of developing emotional and spiritual maturity.

Without conscious engagement, PMS is often reduced to a time when indulging in extra ice cream seems acceptable, rather than being recognized as a valuable, built-in self-therapy mechanism.

It's also worth noting that rules of purity apply to all genders. Apana, the energy responsible for downward movement, exists in every living being, so men too are subject to ritual purity guidelines. Men are advised not to release any sexual fluids before or during puja or homa, whether through voluntary or involuntary ejaculation, with or without contact with women. Additionally, both sexes follow rules regarding illness and the excretion of mucus (e.g., avoiding puja while sick), as these are also processes governed by apana. For more information, consider exploring beliefs around ojas.

In many traditional cultures, customs surrounding menstruation often include not touching women or keeping them in seclusion. To women in the modern world, this may seem extreme and out of place, especially given the demands of balancing work and family life. However, these practices stem from ancient symbolic beliefs about nature and balance.

In Rhythms of Life: Enacting the World with the Goddesses of Orissa, Frederique Apffel-Marglin shares a story from a village in Orissa, India. The women explain that the practice of being "untouchable" during menstruation reflects the natural cycles of the earth and sky. Just as the sky and earth remain separate during the dry season—when there is no rain—menstruation is viewed as a period of separation. The earth, representing the feminine, does not "touch" the sky, symbolizing the masculine, during this time. When the rainy season arrives, the sky and earth reunite, echoing the cycle of fertility and renewal.

In this context, menstrual customs aren't meant to isolate women as impure but to align them with the rhythms of nature. These rituals serve as a reminder of the deep connection between the body, the earth, and the cycles of life. While these traditions may not resonate with everyone today, they reflect a worldview that sees menstruation as part of a larger, sacred order.

A Future Reclaimed

As we reach the end of this journey, one thing is clear: menstruation is more than just a biological process—it is a deeply rooted cultural phenomenon that has shaped and been shaped by societies across time. From ancient fertility rituals to modern-day taboos, the story of menstruation is one of complexity, silence, and, most importantly, power.

By unraveling the myths and folklore, we come to understand how menstruation has been misunderstood, revered, and stigmatized. But today, we stand at a crossroads, where science and tradition can coexist to provide a more complete understanding of the menstrual cycle, fertility, and the female experience.

Now, it is up to us to continue this conversation, to educate the next generation, and to ensure that menstruation is no longer hidden in the shadows. Let us celebrate it as a vital force that connects us to the rhythm of life itself. Through openness, dialogue, and respect, we can create a future where menstruation is embraced as a source of strength, renewal, and empowerment for all.

In recouping menstruation, we reclaim our stories, our bodies, and our voices.

Know Your Author

Dr Sanjhna Nayarr

Dr. Sanjhna Nayarr, Founder and CEO of Safroneya: The Journey Within, is a multifaceted individual—an author, social activist, podcaster, psychic medium, Rune - Numero - Tarot counselor, art therapist, tasseographer, grapho-therapist, and energy healer. She also serves as the National President of the Jewellery and Gems Council at WICCI, Former G100 Oneness and Wisdom Country Advisory Council, and Co-Director of BalikaVidyaArmy, a branch of Project Baalikavidya.

Sanjhna is dedicated to the rights of young girls and women, particularly those who have been victims of human trafficking or rescued from brothels. She also works with children with special needs, such as those with autism, helping to reshape their environment through art therapy. As part of her commitment to women's health, Sanjhna launched a campaign to educate women and girls from the remote regions of north-eastern India, about personal hygiene, introducing and distributing free menstrual cups to empower them to be "period happy," no matter where they live.

She is a proud President's awardee for her service to the community and the upliftment of women, a national award-winning Bharatanatyam artist, and the 2022 recipient of the Best Writer Award for her book Savage Lemonade: An Army Wife's Spiritual Journey. Sanjhna's work has earned her numerous accolades, including the WAOW Warrior Award, the HERA Awards, Centurion of the Year Award, Woman Pioneer Award, Most Inspiring Woman of Earth Award, Exceptional Leader of Excellence Award, IIWA Emerging Woman Author Award, Global Women Inspiring Award, Rashtriya Samaj Seva, and many others, honoring her dedication to social causes and women's empowerment.

www.ingramcontent.com/pod-product-compliance
Lightning Source LLC
LaVergne TN
LVHW041105150826
845673LV00007B/1929
* 9 7 9 8 8 9 5 8 8 5 2 1 5 *